Secrets Never
to be Told

Secrets Never to be Told

Published by The Conrad Press Ltd. in the United Kingdom 2021

Tel: +44(0)1227 472 874
www.theconradpress.com
info@theconradpress.com

ISBN 978-1-914913-20-4

Printed and bound in Great Britain by Clays Ltd, Elcograf S.p.A

Cover Design by Charlotte Mouncey
www.bookstyle.co.uk

Typesetting by The Book Typesetters
www.thebooktypesetters.com

The Conrad Press logo was designed by Maria Priestley.

Secrets Never
to be Told

The true story of a windfall inheritance
and a very personal investigation

Fiona Chesterton

One for Sorrow,
Two for Joy,
Three for a Girl,
Four for a Boy,
Five for Silver,
Six for Gold,
Seven for a Secret
Never to be told

(Traditional rhyme)

Dedicated to Mum and Dad,
to my late husband, Howard,
and to Cousin Jessie.

This is a work of non-fiction and is based on extensive research. However, where persons featured are still living, some names and/or other identifying features have been changed or deliberately omitted.

Contents

List of Illustrations

Prologue

Huntingdon, England, a few days before Christmas, December 2011

I n the end is my beginning.

What happens this quiet weekday December morning appears, on the face of it, to mark the ending of a remarkable story.

Instead, it turns out to be the start of another.

Call it a personal quest, a journey of discovery or even a transformative experience, it begins here in my kitchen, in my house, in a small Cambridgeshire village.

Our post lady Rose finds me, as I usually am these days, at home. She comes to the window and beckons me to go to the back door.

She has a large package, a cardboard box around the size of a small suitcase, for me. As she proffers a delivery form for me to sign, she smiles, wishes me well with my early Christmas present and hands it over.

It is surprisingly light and so is easy to carry inside and place squarely on my old pine table, bleached, scratched and stained as it is by thirty years of family use. I see the postmark of Vancouver and I can guess who sent it.

Sure enough, I find inside a letter from a woman with whom I have been in correspondence for six months now. Mrs Jenkins, Estate Administrator from the Office of the

Public Guardian and Trustee of British Columbia, sent me a bank warrant for 36,000 Canadian dollars a few weeks ago and now has written for the last time.

> Here are memorabilia as promised. Thank you for taking them. Most of the photographs are very old… I am also enclosing a copy of the family tree… We have now closed our file and thank you for your cooperation and assistance.

This, then, was her last act in a case that had been opened the best part of two decades before. It was the end of Mrs Jenkins's work and, as I did not realise yet, the start of mine.

The case that had occupied and, for much of that time foxed, not just Mrs Jenkins but also her predecessors in her office was that of a Canadian man who died in 1994. William Underwood left behind not only a substantial estate but a mystery: he had neither family, friends, nor any birth certificate it seemed.

His mother Jessie, who had died a quarter of a century earlier, was even more of a conundrum. Mrs Jenkins told me it had taken several sets of genealogical detectives to crack where she had come from. They discovered that Jessie had arrived alone on a boat from England nearly a hundred years ago. Within three years of her arrival, William had been born. His father and Jessie's were both unknown. They were both illegitimate and, until this summer, completely unknown to anyone in my family.

It was only in May this year that Mrs Jenkins had finally been able to present a petition to the Supreme Court of

British Columbia and won a decree to distribute William's estate at last to ten beneficiaries. One of them, to my initial consternation and not a little scepticism, was me.

Here now, in the box, in a family tree so painstakingly put together over seventeen years, is the proof of my amazing windfall inheritance. Remarkable as it is, it is not this though that compels my immediate attention. Rather it is the other contents of the box: all that had been left behind by this apparently lonely old man, most bequeathed to him in turn by his mother, Jessie Heading, aka MacDonald, aka Underwood, or as I will call her from this day on, Cousin Jessie.

Here now before me in half a dozen buff-coloured envelopes, labelled in Mrs Jenkins's careful handwriting, are all that remains of my newly found cousin: a birthday book, a few cards and just a couple of letters but lots of photographs. Here, I think, may be a new collection to add to the leather-bound family albums lining a shelf by our stout Victorian front door. As only children, with our parents deceased, my husband Howard and I have become the depository of photos stretching back into the nineteenth century from both sides of our family.

One of the envelopes is marked '*Misc photos taken in Cambridge where Jessie was raised by Harriet*'. I remove them from their envelope, and they spill out onto the table.

They are black and white or sepia prints, of various shapes and sizes, most framed in cardboard, all more than a century old. Some bear the stamp on the corner of the studio where they were taken in the university city just twenty-five miles from where I sit now.

I marvel that they have completed a return journey of many thousands of miles; now in an airfreighted, well-packaged cardboard box, then in a suitcase carrying one woman's worldly goods and all her memories on her long Atlantic journey and cross-continental train ride.

One stands out. It is of a young girl with an older woman in a formal portrait. There is no studio inscription and nothing written on the back, but there is no doubt who it must be: Cousin Jessie, barely into her teens, thirteen or thereabouts by the look of her, with the woman who Mrs Jenkins had told me was not her mother but who had brought her up, a housekeeper called Harriet Rooke.

I look at the Victorian portrait closely. I see in the housekeeper, a Bible in her hand, an epitome of respectability. I notice in her charge a rather long face and a sad expression.

Maybe the photographer had told her to look so solemn, or maybe Jessie was tired of standing still for an inordinately long time. Even so, I doubt from this portrait that she was a happy, laughing, carefree child.

It is the only photograph I can find of Mrs Rooke, and the rest do not form a conventional family collection. Instead, there are pictures of babies and small children plus several portraits of young women. One is a small cameo, which I can identify as an older version of Jessie, with the same long face and expression. A *carte de visite*, I believe the Victorians called such pictures – calling cards.

Amongst the photos, there is one black-framed memorial card. *Thy will be done*, it declares in a Gothic font outside and inside: *In Loving Memory of William Heading, of Sandy, who died November 25th, 1903, aged ninety one years, interred in Morhanger Cemetery.*

The family tree laid out over several pages in another of the envelopes confirms that this William was Jessie's blood grandfather and my maternal great-great-grandfather. This card, which Jessie surely must have treasured, immediately intrigues me, suggesting as it does that Cousin Jessie knew something of her true origins.

Of her origins, and so of her shame.

Jessie bore the enduring shame of the illegitimate child, passed in the mother's milk, a curdled concoction indeed. William Heading's daughter Mary Ann gave birth to Jessie in 1877 and had, it seemed, never married, nor borne another child, paying apparently a lifelong penalty for her crime. There is no photograph of her in the box.

I pause a moment and think of my own mother, another Mary. We are coming up to only the third Christmas I will have spent without her. Until her death, I had always been with her then. For the first twenty-five years of my life we were together in the Midlands city of Leicester, where Mum and I were both born, she in the middle of the First World War, me in the 'baby boomer' years following the Second.

My sense of loss though is not the reason for the bittersweet feeling I have right now – rather, it is reflecting on what she shared with her nineteenth-century namesake. You see, Mum was a woman who also had a child out of wedlock in an era barely less censorious than the Victorian.

That child, dear Reader, was me.

I share more than genes with Cousin Jessie and her apparently unlawful child. As for my mum, I reckon she carried a lifelong penalty too.

I return from my thoughts to the buff envelopes and move quickly through the thin one labelled William Underwood to one marked George Underwood. Mrs Jenkins has told me that he had briefly been Jessie's husband and had given the boy his name but was not the boy's father. Mrs Jenkins was quite adamant on that point. There are many more photos here too but none to interest me immediately.

I move quickly on again to the next, labelled Jessie Heading Underwood, which contains yet more photographs. They were taken, it would seem in Canada, in the 1920s in what looks like a prosperous prairie community in British Columbia.

At the bottom of this pile is one picture that arrests my attention, a picture that comes to haunt me. It is a large one, framed in a funereal brown cardboard and without inscription.

A woman is standing with a small boy in a field, in front of what I think at first is a tumbledown farm building. Then I notice the chimney and realise that it is a small dwelling, little better than a shack. There is a bicycle in the long grass immediately in front of it and some planks of wood in a small pile alongside the bike.

The woman standing in front of this dwelling has to be Jessie – and the boy, surely, is William. The grass – or is it wheat? – comes up to his waist, so you can only see his shirt and the top of his dungarees.

He looks about seven years old, which I work out would date the photo to 1922. He is attempting a smile, while Jessie has a shy, uncomfortable expression. Her eyes are half-closed, perhaps against the glare of the sun. She is wearing a plain workaday outfit, with a long skirt more redolent of a previous era.

It looks as if the photographer has disturbed her briefly from her domestic toil. There are no pictures of Jessie here in her Sunday-best nor in more relaxed mode; nor is there a single photo of her with George – not even a wedding photograph.

I notice the absence of that particularly. I notice – and remember.

Leicester, England, 1962

I am sitting on the sofa and staring at the stone mantelpiece. Or rather I am staring at the absence of something on the mantelpiece.

A wedding photograph.

My parents did not have much in the way of sitting room adornment; there was no glazed cabinet to display the best china nor side table with family photographs, such as my aunts and uncles had. There was a rather gloomy print reproduction in a gilt frame of a seventeenth-century Dutch domestic scene over the fireplace and the occasional seaside postcard brightened the brown marbled top, propped up against the battery-driven clock in its faux walnut case.

So, for the untrained eye, the absence of a photograph of Mum and Dad smiling at the camera outside the church door or Register Office in best suit and wedding dress might not have been remarkable.

For me, though, used to spending many hours on my own in that room, it begins to assume a great significance. I am ten years old and beginning to learn the ways of the world at school.

One of my class, a girl called Cherry with enviable long chestnut-brown hair, was a subject of some pity amongst my classmates as it seemed her parents were divorced and she lived alone with her mother. Divorce was something extraordinary, featuring occasionally in the newspapers, but not something that was part of everyday life in a city in the Midlands of England in the austere post-war middle years of the twentieth century.

I am also beginning to learn, mainly from reading the Sunday papers, about domestic scandals and the concept of adultery. These things simply do not happen in my world nor that of my classmates.

I am yet to learn about unmarried mothers, teenage pregnancies, and what being a bastard meant... and quite how close to home these could be.

It takes me a while to summon up the courage to raise the subject of the photograph – or lack of photograph – with my mum. Her answer does not convince me nor settle my anxieties. Something like, they didn't bother with such things.

In a drawer, there is a pile of black and white snaps that my dad had taken of me with his Kodak camera when we went on our annual seaside holiday to Bridlington or on our very occasional day trips. There are also studio photos framed in white card of me as a baby, including one with a Coronation crown crest and holly-framed photos taken of me in my uniform at my school's annual pre-Christmas session.

Then there are those taken by seaside photographers of me walking along the prom with a bucket and spade, often in a coat or jumper suitable for what they called 'bracing' summer weather on the North Sea coast. The most recent of these is a photo of me in a summer dress, again taken on holiday, with a monkey on my arm.

By comparison, there are only a few pictures of my mother and father together before I was born and a couple of my father on the cricket pitch of the Buckinghamshire village that my mother told me they had lived in for a few years before they settled down again in Leicester. There are no wedding photographs in that pile either, framed or unframed.

I become convinced I am adopted. I must have read about adopted children somewhere. Perhaps in Dickens or in the *Daily Mirror*.

To the modern reader, it may seem extraordinary that a ten-year-old would have jumped to this conclusion, rather than the one that now in hindsight is so obvious and which I never imagined – because mums and dads in my experience were always married.

My mother is quick to dispel my fear that I am not her child. She tells me where I was born, in Leicester General Hospital. To her. The place she'd worked in the war. I find this account more persuasive but not conclusive.

Why am I an only child?

That was another awkward question I ask. Mummy, as I called her then, had not wanted any more than one, she says.

Just one child, to whom they could give all their love and all their resources and energy on bringing up.

I have no doubt at all that I am loved. Still, I dream of having an older brother. Someone who could chaperone me and allow me to go on adventures outside of the house, to go places and do things together. I was sure they would allow a boy more freedom than I had.

You see, I feel I am in a cage, designed not only to keep me safe, but also, I suspect, to prevent my mixing with 'common' people as they were called then (we live in a working-class area of Leicester).

It is, though, a cage gilded in my parents' love. I am the centre of their world.

Somehow my parents found the money to send me to a private primary school in Stoneygate, one of the best areas of the city. I am driven there in the morning and driven home after school.

Now that I am ten, it has dawned on me that it is odd and not normal, that I am neither allowed out at all on my own nor spend any time outside school with other children. I play alone in our unkempt and grass-free back yard, with the chicken coop and the regular rumble of the trains of the Great Central line beyond the garden wall.

The street is out of bounds except for weekly trips to the fish and chip shop on the corner. Mummy and I occasionally walk over to see her sisters in Belgrave via Rushey Fields, which is the nearest park, but I am not allowed to venture to playgrounds on my own.

It's hardly surprising then that I have grown fat – or 'chubby', as my mum prefers to call it. That picture of me with the monkey makes me cringe, not because of the abuse of animals, which was not questioned then, but because of the size of me.

I am not allowed school friends to tea, let alone for sleepovers (which are not a thing in the Sixties anyway). I do not have birthday parties, although they are rarer then too.

We do not go to church. Mummy does not approve of the Brownies – they are too militaristic, she says when I ask.

All the expeditions outside the house, mainly for shopping, are with Mummy or Daddy, only rarely with both of them.

Occasionally, I am allowed to go next door, where Daddy works as the manager at the Working Men's Club. There is a big stage upstairs and entertainers of all kinds – singers, magicians, comedians and novelty turns, I'm told – perform in a packed, smoke-filled room here on Saturday night.

I only walk onto that stage when it is empty on a weekday morning and I can just dream of performing there. I start singing:

'Some…Where over the Rainbow'

I hear the oddly hollow acoustic.

'Way up High.'

You see, I love singing, dancing, acting – any sort of performance.

I go every week to a speech coach and win medals for reciting poetry and reading aloud. My mother tells me that I had a speech impediment diagnosed when I started school and had been recommended therapy. My first school report indeed recorded that the kindergarten teacher had trouble understanding what I said.

As well as dealing with that, my elocution classes with

'Madame' Rothery are also removing the broad and not very melodious East Midlands accent that I would otherwise develop. As George Bernard Shaw famously noted, you judge the class of an Englishwoman as soon as she opens her mouth.

Mummy is an even rarer visitor to the club, where my dad works six days a week, including every weekend. At the age of ten, I am only beginning to understand that her life is stunted too.

She also is in a cage, but one of her own making, it seems. She does not go to work – well, that's not unusual, of course, although Leicester is a city where very many married women go out to work in the hosiery and shoe factories.

She rarely goes out alone during the day and hardly ever in the evening with my father, on his one night off. Occasionally, she goes without me to visit her sisters and a brother, who still live in the McDonald family house where she had been brought up, or to see some of her other siblings, who live walking distance away.

Those on the other side of town and the brother who moved away, she sees more rarely. She has no interest in learning to drive, even though it would make seeing them easier.

It's not just logistics that make it difficult to keep in regular touch with her family. I sense there is a rift of some sort, some long-running sore that I feel goes back to before I was born.

My mother mentions some dispute over her parents' will, that of my McDonald grandparents. Maybe that accounts for it.

Maybe. But it can't account for the fact that Daddy is also

inexplicably estranged from his family.

I don't truly realise yet that my mother is not happy in her cage. That only dawns on me a year later – in 1963, the year I pass my eleven-plus and go to grammar school.

The year the Beatles bring joy and mania to me and to most eleven-year-old girls.

The year when my reading of the *Daily Mirror* brings new revelations of what some very exotic adults get up to, with the Profumo scandal and the Duchess of Argyll's divorce case (the one with the infamous 'headless' man, whose identity was the subject of frenzied gossip – a Hollywood star or a member of the Royal Family perhaps).

That was the year that was, 1963, the year the Swinging Sixties started in London, a world away.

The year that led inexorably to my mother's first nervous breakdown.

Huntingdon, 2011

This cardboard box contains so much more than just the miscellaneous memorabilia of a distant cousin. In opening it, a great deal more than a pile of photographs will come spilling out.

The first flicker of what will become a burning desire to make sense of these fragments of Jessie's long life, somehow to reassess mine, sparks inside me. I will need to understand what drove Jessie to escape England and travel thousands of miles alone – for what?

To have a child out of wedlock, compounding that shame – and burden – into a third generation?

To marry an old man? To live in a shack?

I will need to go on my own journey to try to find the answers; not as a mere curiosity, trying to rediscover a world that no longer exists, but for something much more vivid and urgent.

You see, like Jessie, I sense I changed my identity to survive the stigma of being a love child – or rather, I believe my parents were determined to create a new identity for me. They did this so effectively that I did not discover their – and my – secret until I was in my mid-forties – strangely, at about the same age that Jessie was in the prairie photograph that has so enthralled me.

In uncovering Jessie's story, I feel that I will be freed for the first time to tell mine… but not quite yet. Life is too overwhelming right now. You see, I am home as I have given up work to care for my husband, who is increasingly disabled.

We have learnt just a few months ago that his illness is terminal. My windfall inheritance we regard as a godsend to provide us with an insurance in case the increasing nursing costs we may face come to exhaust our savings.

There is no more time now to sit looking at old photographs. I hear my husband, with his failing voice, calling me.

I must go.

Chapter One

Cambridge, England, 2015

There's no going back now.

After nearly two years of navigating the perils of the property market, I have managed to sell the family house in the country, where I lived for more than twenty years. I have bought a new, smaller place in Cambridge.

I am a widow now and have to rebuild my life on my own, sink or swim. I decided I needed a city again to do that. Cambridge was not my heart's desire but would do – no, more than do. Moving here will give me the opportunity to discover more about Cousin Jessie in the place where she lived as a child and young woman.

The window the windfall inheritance opened so unexpectedly on a family secret four years ago had been firmly shut, my days taken up with caring for my dying husband. Its pinprick of light on a distant and alluring world disappeared in the all-consuming darkness. Now the time is right to open that window again.

The box of memorabilia and the correspondence from Mrs Jenkins of Vancouver re-emerge from the packing cases. Rather than putting them away in a cupboard, I place them on a shelf in my new kitchen, where I can be reminded daily of the distant cousin who had sparked something in my imagination, something very real and very personal.

I hope to re-create Cousin Jessie, a woman who had been rescued from oblivion, having been lost to my family for more than a hundred years. I will do that in order to validate her life, one that could well have been limited to being a richer man's servant, with only a licence to sleep in the bed where she laid her head. Instead she became an independent, property-owning woman – and against the odds, it seemed.

I sit at my old pine table, now transported into its new home where the stains and scratches stand out even more in the pristine white surroundings. I open the file and read again that first astonishing letter.

Dated June 13, 2011 and postmarked Vancouver, it was addressed to me as executor of my late mother's estate. It came from an organisation that, until then, I had never heard of: The Office of the Public Guardian and Trustee of British Columbia.

I was surprised it had even reached me, as the envelope bore a long-out-of-date postcode. My initial surprise had turned rapidly to suspicion.

'Re the Estate of the Late William Underwood,' it declared.

I had never heard of him.

'Our office is administering the estate of the above deceased who died on September 11, 1994.'

This line in the letter had looked the most suspicious of all. Was I to believe that it had taken more than a decade and a half to contact me?

'The gross value of the estate is approximately $358,000.00. Please note that we have now obtained a Court Order of Distribution dated May 30, 2011 issued by the Supreme Court of British Columbia in favour of the following ten heirs.'

On the list of those to receive a tenth share are some familiar and unfamiliar names, and in bold, my mother's name.

The letter continued to a second page. I was required to send a copy of the probate documents of my mother's estate to this Canadian office – but no cash, I noted.

This incredible letter was signed with an indecipherable squiggle. Typed beneath was the name of Mrs Jenkins, Estate Administrator. A direct line; a fax number; an email address.

Well, what would you have made of such a letter? Too good to be true, perhaps?

I rang one of my cousins, whose mother's name was also on the list. A doctor, very sensible.

She reckoned it might be a scam. Yes, her mother, then a frail ninety-year-old, told her last year, shortly before she died, that she'd received a call from a very well-spoken gentleman – a man with a title, apparently – to tell her that she was coming into some money. She thought that was a scam too and had told her mum to forget about it.

Well, I am glad now we gave Mrs Jenkins the chance to prove her credentials. I'd sent the Canadian official a cautious, bordering on hostile, reply to her letter, demanding she offer evidence of her bona fides. In response, she stated simply:

'Please be assured this is not a scam.'

She gave me the names of the Canadian solicitor who had dealt with the case and the details of the genealogical company, heir hunters as they are often called, to help convince me.

So it was that I found myself talking to the very same gentleman, let's call him Sir Q, who ran the firm, and who I was sure as soon as he started speaking must be the man my recently deceased aunt had spoken to.

He had a cut-glass English upper-class accent. I immediately got the impression that he wasn't likely to give me a lot of his time.

He confirmed he'd spoken to my aunt and that his company had been retained to locate and document William Underwood's next of kin. That involved, he said, going back several generations to what was an unknown and illegitimate branch of my mother's family. Indeed, not one but two levels of illegitimacy were involved.

Was there just a hint of disapproval in his voice at this revelation, or was I imagining it? Sir Q sounded of mature years, so I feared might share those old prejudices.

Why had it taken quite so long to track us all down? the still-sceptical me asked.

The gentleman genealogist explained that it took a long time to trace us, as Canadian records in the early twentieth century – well, they were simply not up to British standards, he said, with the weariness and frustration of many hours' heir-hunting in colonial archives.

Yes, I thought, but seventeen years? Really?

So why hadn't all my cousins been beneficiaries? I asked. I had many, as my mother was one of eleven children.

He explained that some were disqualified, their parents having pre-deceased William. That was the somewhat brutal law of intestacy, I learned.

He seemed to know what he was talking about but this

aristocratic detective still seemed implausible to me. I expressed some scepticism as to whether this was for real. Maybe the word 'scam' passed my lips. That was a mistake. Sir Q very soon brought the call to a close.

Remembering that difficult phone conversation four years ago, I now wonder if I might do better a second time and could brave another encounter. I looked up Sir Q and it seemed he was still pursuing the heir-hunting trade.

I rehearsed what I might say to him this time. How I was pleased that he had helped resolve the case... How I was curious to find out more about Jessie and William... to learn more about this Canadian wing of the family. Could I ask him a few questions? Perhaps come to see him?

I picked up the phone. An unmistakable voice answered.

I started on my rehearsed lines but did not get far.

I'm afraid I can't help – that was his blunt message, covered with a polite veneer. Sir Q seemed even keener than he had been a few years earlier to curtail the conversation. It was clear that he had neither forgotten, nor forgiven, the accusation of being party to a scam.

I suppose I should not have been surprised. Well, I would have to do my own research but how was I going to begin?

I thought I'd try Mrs Jenkins as we had ended up on very good terms, after my initial *froideur*. I'd had no contact with her since that Christmas package four years ago and an email now went unanswered. Maybe she had retired or taken a new job, having closed the protracted case of Mr William Underwood.

Rather than try to track her down or seek out whoever might have succeeded her at the Office of the Public

Guardian, I decide not to make any approach as yet. I think I might get further if I do some basic research myself, so as to know what further questions to ask. That was how I would have approached an investigation, if I had been plying my old journalist's trade rather than this very personal project.

So, as a starting point for my own inquiries, I marshal all the information Mrs Jenkins had given me. I check my computer archive and recover the first digital message I received from her.

Email sent Tuesday July 12, 2011, 4.43 p.m.:

'Jessie Ashpole Heading was the illegitimate daughter of Mary Ann Heading. We do not know the identity of Jessie's father… Jessie came to Canada around 1903 [sic]. She was single and travelling alone…

William Underwood was born on March 5, 1915, in New Westminster B.C. He was the illegitimate son of Jessie Ashpole MacDonald (Heading). We have been unable to locate a birth registration for William Underwood so we do not know the identity of the father…

Jessie Ashpole MacDonald (Heading) married George Underwood in 1920 when William was about five years old. George was not William's biological father.'

Well, that was a lot to double-check for a start. I know already there's one mistake, maybe a typing error: Jessie arrived in Canada in 1912 not 1903.

Then there are so many names to check! How could I ever have imagined that a scammer could have dreamt this up?

Yet this was the barest summary of their lives and hardly scratched the surface of the story I wished to know. My motivation for pursuing this is quite different from the previous official researchers.

Their task was straightforward, if difficult to achieve. They simply had to find a person or persons with a bona fide claim to William's estate and prove it to the satisfaction of the court.

My objective is more complex and I know could be even more challenging. I want to find out who Jessie was.

Questions come thick and fast into my mind. How had a young woman in Edwardian England become so desperate – or perhaps in such need of adventure – that she had left everything she knew behind her and travelled to another continent on her own?

How had she come to be alone with a child, apparently conceived and born illegitimately in Canada? Why had she, a town dweller in England, ended up on the prairie?

Through what good fortune had she, a poor servant woman, managed not just to make an independent living but come to bequeath a property to her son, an asset worth some $350,000 by William's death in 1994? With inflation, its value would be at least double that now, I reckoned.

Then, for me, is the biggest question of all: had Cousin Jessie's life been defined by illegitimacy – or had it been the making of her?

To answer those questions – assuming it is even possible – I will need to use every clue in the Christmas box that Mrs Jenkins sent me. I will need to follow those clues with some proper research, online and in the real world.

I will need to go to Canada before too long, that's for sure. Yes, I will use some of that money I inherited to go to British Columbia.

Go find that field in the prairie where Cousin Jessie stood

with her boy to have her picture taken. Yes, do that – and hope to pay my respects at her final resting place.

To think, this quest would have all been so much simpler if I had had a chance to ask Jessie herself, when she was an old woman and I, a curious child! Our lives had overlapped by all of eighteen years. If our circumstances had been different, maybe she could have told me her life story, overcoming Victorian reticence and nearly a century of secrecy in the freer air of her new country.

Well, maybe now in the twenty-first century, but as I think back, it would have been a pretty impossible encounter the best part of a lifetime ago – and a world away.

Leicester, 1962

I am lying in a darkened room, in my parents' bed, not my own.

They must be sleeping in the front room next door, in what they call the Z-bed, which is a foldable mattress in a wooden frame, kept along with the junk in there. As we hardly ever get visitors and never overnight ones, I have no idea why this bed has been kept.

It can't be very comfortable for Mummy and Daddy in there. The floorboards are bare, as is the lightbulb, and there's no fire. There are nets at the windows to keep out prying eyes from the upper floor of the house over the road – and that's all.

Mummy never speaks to the neighbours, neither those

opposite, nor in the house next door. Net curtains seem to be her first line of defence against a world that should be kept firmly at bay.

I have the measles, am off school and very bored. I must have caught it at school as I don't spend time with other children. I have never seen any playing in the street here but even if there were some, I would never get to meet them.

Mummy says I have to keep the light off – she says I could go blind if I turn it on. So I lie under the bedclothes in the gloom with just a little transistor radio to keep me company.

It is tuned to Radio Luxembourg – 'Your Station of the Stars', as they nightly proclaim – and I listen avidly. Through the crackle, the music is still more exciting than what's on the Light Programme. There's a new record called 'Love Me Do' by a group called the Beatles that I like a lot and it is sure to be played at least once every night.

Between the music and the disc jockey patter, there is also a man called Horace Batchelor from a place called Keynsham, advertising some way of winning money on the football pools. I don't think my dad, who fills in his Littlewoods coupon every week, has much time for him though. He thinks it's a scam.

During the day, it is still pretty gloomy with the curtains drawn. I can't read and there is nothing to play with.

The big wardrobe – made of a browny-pink, shiny, composite material – and its matching dressing table might offer me some entertainment if I were allowed out of bed. Mummy keeps a beautiful hairbrush, comb and mirror set on the pearly table top, as well as a powder puff in a small china box and a cut-glass perfume bottle with a gold-tasselled spray handle. As the bottle is empty and the brush immaculate, this collection seems for decoration rather than use.

The wardrobe is full of possibilities too. On the left side, where my mother's clothes are kept, there is a fur coat, several beautiful dresses and a suit, with a couple of pairs of high-heeled shoes and matching leather handbags.

I have never seen Mummy wear any of these alluring items. I know from reading her *Woman's Own* that they are not in the current style, more in the New Wave fashion of a decade or more ago.

There are a few photos of Mummy in the drawer – smartly dressed, her raven-coloured hair styled, her face made up with powder and lipstick – but it feels to me as if that woman has been shelved, filed away along with the clothes here in this wardrobe.

I would never dare try any of them on, for fear of spoiling their pristine perfection. From time to time, I do risk trying on the shoes and teeter around the bedroom in them. Not now, though; the wardrobe doors are firmly shut and the daytime hours drag by more than the evening ones do.

I am impatient to get better and go back to school. It's not long till I am due to sit the eleven-plus. Mummy and Daddy have their heart set on my passing and going to grammar school, so I don't want to miss classes.

It didn't matter so much when I was younger, when my less than satisfactory attendance record was noted, as I had endless winter colds that often turned into bronchitis. Mummy kept me away from school for a week or even two to recover. That's before the other diseases, like the chickenpox, mumps, German measles and, worst of all, the whooping cough.

Mummy says I nearly ended up in hospital with that, although I can't remember it at all. I think she worries that our living beside the railway line doesn't help my health either. That's also why she insists Daddy hardly smokes at all in the house, so he gets through most of his two packets a day in the Club next door.

All I want to do now is to get back to normal – to daylight, the curtains opened wide – and to my own room across the corridor.

I like my bedroom. It overlooks the railway line, where sometimes I can wave at the people in the carriages.

Where are they off to, I wonder? To the seaside, perhaps, or to London, to see the Queen or the Houses of Parliament? The whole wide world surely lies over my back fence, courtesy of the engines of the Great Central Railway.

Amongst the treasures and toys in my bedroom is a large globe, which I can turn and turn to see the world. The country I live in is barely bigger than my little finger but the pink in which it is coloured is replicated on whole swathes of the land mass on this globe.

On the continent of North America, it seems, close to half of it is pink. Canada's vastness stretches from the very top of the world southwards till it meets the equally vast but proudly un-pink United States.

Will I go there one day?

It seems a pretty remote possibility. Mummy has never left the country in her whole life, not even to Scotland or Ireland, and Daddy says he saw enough of the world to satisfy him for a lifetime in the war.

I can dream, though, as I watch the old movies on the

television on Sunday afternoons. I love the musicals best, especially those featuring Fred Astaire and Ginger Rogers. I twirl around with them in the small space between the television, the fireplace and the sofa.

Maybe if I keep up with my ballet classes at school – and change shape and not grow too tall – that could be a way to get to this glamourous world of satin shoes and silk ballgowns, of sequins and feathers, peopled with women like Ginger. She not only dances with magical skill but has an endless line in witty rejoinders to the charming but irritatingly bumptious Fred.

Still, even now, I am beginning to realise that the Hollywood of my dreams is a fantasy, as much a one as the Narnia, Middle Earth and Looking Glass worlds of the books on my bedroom shelf.

Those dreams were punctured this summer with the news, relayed on one of those Hollywood Sunday afternoons, that Marilyn Monroe had died. The most beautiful woman in the world was found lying in her Californian bedroom, an empty bottle of tablets by her lifeless side.

Death became real to me this year not just because of the peerless Marilyn, but also because of my Uncle Hec. He was the first member of Mummy's family who had died since I was born. Hector was her oldest brother, sixteen years her senior but still only sixty-two when he had a heart attack.

Mummy told me her earliest memory was of him coming home from the Belgian trenches in 1918. She said she was so frightened by this stranger in a uniform that she ran into her mother's long skirts to hide.

Hector McDonald had a beautiful tenor voice; I heard it

just the once and never forgot it. Mummy said there was talk of him going to Italy to train for the opera when he was a young man but that was as out of reach to him then as the West Coast of America feels to me now. He ran a sweet shop in Leicester instead.

I cried when I heard that he died. We hadn't visited often but I loved it when we did.

Occasionally Daddy would go with Uncle Hec to see a football match and Mummy and I would stay talking with Auntie Ida until they came back. Then, before we went home, I could have my pick from the rows of glass jars containing sweets of every colour and shape, filling up a large white paper bag and taking a chocolate bar too.

The sweet shop and Auntie are still there, I know, but without Uncle Hec it seems a fearful place. As I lie in my sickbed in the darkened room, I sense his ghost is very close, only kept at bay by the crackle of Radio Luxembourg.

Don't tell me ghosts don't exist. I hear his voice, I see him on the stairs.

At night, there are dark, cold and silent places in this house, where spirits could lurk. Mummy says she believes in ghosts too – maybe those are the ghosts of her past life.

Cambridge, 2015

I begin. I remove the family tree from its buff envelope carefully labelled by Mrs Jenkins and spread it out on my new kitchen floor.

There are six A4 pages that only make sense laid out end to end. It doesn't have my name and my generation on it; it starts with my mother's.

I see such a complex grid of names. Of course, until relatively recently, English families tended to have lots of children. Mum's was certainly one of those.

I do a quick count up from the bottom row where my mum's name, Mary Chesterton, *née* McDonald, is recorded along with all ten of her siblings. There are one, two, three, four generations going back to my maternal great-great-grandparents.

Here they are at the top of this tree: William Heading and his wife Sarah, born in the Napoleonic era and married in 1841 when Victoria was still a young queen. They are Cousin Jessie's natural grandparents. It is this William whose memorial card, once amongst Jessie's treasured possessions, is now amongst mine.

Across the spread pages I can see a surprising number of redactions, obscuring most of the names of spouses. For data protection, I suppose, although whose privacy could possibly be breached by revealing these century-old marriages, I can't imagine.

There are still quite a few names I recognise. Lots of McDonalds, for a start. The one highest up the chart is my great-grandfather John Moore McDonald, who married one of William Heading's daughters.

Along that row, my eye settles on the name of another one of his daughters: Mary Ann Heading, Cousin Jessie's natural mother. There was no spousal name redacted here; she had never married. Born 1851, died Christmas Eve 1933, I read.

So that meant that she was still alive long after Jessie had gone to Canada and that Jessie was her only child. My mind computes the sad implications of that.

There's one name I can't find on this chart – that of Mrs Harriet Rooke, Jessie's adoptive mother. I can't see anything here to explain how she fitted into the picture.

I am already testing some hypotheses in my mind but I tell myself to be methodical and not let my imagination run ahead of my reasoning. First things first. Let's see if I can find out more about how Jessie came to be born and then given away.

It is easy to find Mary Ann Heading online, not just in the birth and death records but also in a series of censuses. She lived with her father William on a farm in the Old Warden area of Bedfordshire for much of her life. By 1881, four years after she'd given birth to her only child in Cambridge, she was back living with him.

I see there was also a child in the household then, a boy of the same age as Jessie. He had the extraordinary name of Original Heading Mackness.

A check with the family tree tells me that this lad was Mary Ann's nephew, another sister's child. So it looks like Mary Ann gave up her own baby and cared for her sister's – a girl traded for a boy, it seems.

I think of that old rhyme: one for sorrow, two for joy, three for a girl, four for a boy. A boy child counted for more.

I kept following Mary Ann's trail into the twentieth century. Ever the spinster, she was still living with her father William in 1901 but now, instead of Original, there was another young man living with them, one John McDonald, son of my great-grandfather.

Hadn't Mrs Jenkins said something to me about this McDonald having some role in Jessie's life? I would need to check that out later.

Another decade on and the records show me that William Heading was dead, John had married, and Mary Ann was living 'with private means' in the company of other elderly single women in the town of Sandy.

There was no sign at all in these records that she had ever lived or been to Cambridge, let alone had a child there. The official record depicted a quiet life with no hint of scandal, nor any thing remarkable at all. She was one of the legions of maiden aunts, as they were called then, living respectable lives of what seems now like unbearable tedium. A lot of tea in fine china cups was surely drunk.

Yet I knew that somehow at the not giddy age of twenty-five, Mary Ann had had a baby in Cambridge; an event she may have gone to some lengths to hide but that she certainly would not have forgotten. What heartbreak, sorrow or shame was that, swept under the carpet?

What subterfuge was there to disguise the pregnancy? What consolation might there have been in nurturing her sister's surplus but useful boy child instead of her own little girl, whom she had handed over to the care of a middle-aged housekeeper?

I sit at a computer screen in the public library, quietly fuming at the injustice of Jessie's fate. I need to take a break from the library and take a trip.

I drive to Old Warden one Sunday afternoon to find the Headings' Victorian farmhouse still standing. It lies hidden less than a mile as the crow flies from the A1, at the point where a Sainsbury's superstore forms a landmark in these Bedfordshire flatlands.

I turn off the main road and drive tentatively up an unmarked and potholed track. I park the car by the side of the road and continue up on foot towards the farm. It looks like a substantial and still occupied private property.

I am brought to a halt, though, by two 'Keep Out' signs. To my left, I see fencing and barbed wire surrounding what looks like a flooded gravel pit.

Then some fierce-sounding dogs start barking. I take a couple of photos but decide not to ring the bell.

Returning to the car, I look at a map and see that the site of the home of Mary Ann's older sister, my great-grandmother Elizabeth McDonald, is not far away but after winding down a few more country lanes, I abandon the search.

I have seen enough to conclude that these Victorian farming families, even in areas close to the main staging road between London and the north of England, would have been pretty self-sufficient and, if need be, could have kept some family secrets firmly behind closed doors.

Back in Cambridge, I return to the library. One Saturday morning I sit down at a computer with one of the volunteer helpers there, who shows me how to search the recently digitised parish records.

I am already learning that you can have a frustrating time with genealogy when you go back to the nineteenth century, particularly if you are dealing with ordinary people, especially women, who usually change their surnames.

You can easily get misled by mis-recorded handwritten data or just carried away by wrong assumptions. You can run into dead ends too and frustrating omissions.

Or you can get lucky. As I do this morning.

Here in the records of All Saints, a church that still stands proud in the very centre of Cambridge, my helper finds an entry that plainly reveals to me one of the secrets that was surely kept from Jessie all her long life and that the Office of the Public Guardian and their genealogical detectives had failed to uncover even with seventeen years to do so.

Here it was: a baptism dated February 10, 1877.

The baby, 'Jessie Ashbowl [*sic*] Heading,' born a few weeks earlier.

The mother, Mary Ann Heading, address 66 Sidney Street, Cambridge, daughter of a Bedfordshire farmer...

and the name of Jessie's father: Richard Ashbowl Crisp, currently of the same Cambridge address, also from Bedfordshire and also a farmer.

Paternity had been declared to God if not to man, as Mrs Jenkins had told me that Jessie's birth certificate had no father's name. It seemed that this man had given his middle name to Jessie, if little else.

A library is not the usual place for excitement, but that is what I feel this morning. I want to hug that volunteer. With her quiet skills, digging out a now digitised record, which it would seem was not available to the Canadian researchers nor the formidable Sir Q, we have cracked a secret kept for more than one hundred and forty years.

I can hardly wait to find out more about this man. I track Richard Crisp down easily enough in the 1871 census. At that time, he was a bachelor in his mid-twenties living with his mother, a widow, in their family farmhouse in a place called Northill, which lies just a short horse ride away from the Headings' farm.

So in the spring of 1876, when Jessie was conceived, Richard, aged thirty, and Mary Ann, five years younger, seem to have been free to marry. I can only speculate why they didn't.

A family feud? I knew all about the virulence of those from my twenty years living in a village.

A father's or mother's disapproval?

Or something darker...? But if it had been a case of rape, would Richard have accompanied Mary Ann to Cambridge?

All questions I already know I can never answer. Still, discovering the name of Jessie's father feels like a good omen to me. I've only just started – and already I feel that Cousin Jessie's other secrets may soon be revealed to me too.

Chapter Two

Cambridge, 2016

There have always been at least two Cambridges.

There's the one the tourists and students know, the one dominated by the colleges of the university, with their medieval courts and lawns sweeping down to the River Cam and the Backs, the one featuring the glories of King's College Chapel, the Bridge of Sighs and the Mathematical Bridge, the punts and the cream teas. Despite its attempted contemporary rebranding as the hub of 'Silicon Fen', this traditional Cambridge still dominates – all part of that Britain we can't quite relinquish, which brings in the tourist dollar – increasingly the yen and the yuan – and which links Oxbridge to *Downton Abbey* in our collective imaginations and worldview.

As a new resident, a walk around the historic heart of the city, especially on a sunny day, still bewitches. The old colleges with their grand façades make it all too easy to imagine the scene when Richard Crisp and Mary Ann Heading arrived here some one hundred and forty years ago.

Still, it was not into that sunlit world of privilege that Cousin Jessie was born, but into the other Cambridge – the town, rather than the gown, which has long lived cheek by jowl but is much less well known. Jessie arrived in the dead, cold month of January 1877 in the lodgings at No. 66 Sidney

Street, which her mother shared, at least for a while, with her father.

It was just a stone's throw from Christ's College, whose most famous alumnus, Charles Darwin, would be awarded the honorary degree of Doctor of Laws for his revolutionary scientific work later that year. Indeed, when Darwin had first arrived in Cambridge as a student nearly fifty years earlier, he had initially taken lodgings in the very same terrace in Sidney Street, home now to Boots the Chemist.

I spot the commemorative plaque set halfway up the stonework above the store's modern fascia, then stand and wonder how this country couple came to lodge here. Maybe Richard Ashbowl Crisp had a friend at one of the colleges or perhaps the contact was through farming or horse-riding friends who helped him find rooms to rent. It might have also been through these contacts that they found the kindly woman prepared to adopt their baby.

I have found out much about Hattie Rooke, born Harriet Fromant, from local records. She came from a family of blacksmiths who lived in villages on the Newmarket side of Cambridge, an area now synonymous with horse-breeding and racing, of course.

She was born in the village of Swaffham Bulbeck and came into town as a young woman to work in service. She married the son of a stud groom called Alfred Rooke, who worked in a Cambridge tavern as an ostler looking after the horses. It was a short-lived marriage, however, and by 1877 she was a forty-two-year-old widow.

As I could not find any family connection between her family and either the Crisps or the Headings, I concluded that the arrangement for her to bring up Jessie was most likely a straightforward commercial transaction. Mrs Rooke, already past what was seen then as her prime, on her own and childless, no doubt saw this as a good opportunity – not just to have a child, but for a steady income from a regular Bedfordshire cheque to supplement her earnings from housekeeping. A girl, moreover, could offer the prospect of both consolation and companionship in her widowhood, becoming in just a few years an assistant with the housework and eventually bringing in extra income on her own account.

Maybe Richard Crisp thought he was doing the right thing by Mary Ann and their new baby by taking them to Cambridge, and no doubt he encouraged the arrangement with Mrs Rooke, especially if Grandpa Heading was prepared to pick up the bill.

For Mary Ann, a return to the farm, her beloved family, and her sister's child to nurture offered a more secure life than any she might have had in the alien bustle, dirt, noise and damp of a Victorian market town.

Her father William might well have been a forgiving man – or at least practical – perhaps pledging to support his granddaughter as penance for preferring to take into his home a lawful boy rather than an illicit girl.

For Richard Crisp, it was certainly a good arrangement. By 1881, he had started a new life with his mother in the Bletchley area of Buckinghamshire, working as a farm bailiff.

Whether it was the scandal of the baby that caused him to leave Northill, or one of the periodic recessions in farming that forced him out, I could only guess. What was certain was that five years later he married, and within a decade had four legitimate children. He had clearly put the affair with Mary Ann firmly behind him.

Mrs Rooke meanwhile got work as a housekeeper in one of the new houses in the rapidly developing Mill Road area of the town. South-east of the large common of Parker's Piece, and close to the railway sidings, it was a hive of industrial activity, of shops and workshops, of pubs and churches and chapels.

It was also home to the Cambridge workhouse, the end of the road for so many poor Victorians and a monument of moral warning to those men – and especially to those women – who fell from grace through what was deemed wanton and feckless behaviour, or a surfeit of gin or opium, or both. The workhouse was also handily situated close to the new sprawling cemetery – the graveyard, next to the graveyard of hopes.

The first household Mrs Rooke and the infant Jessie moved into was on the more respectable side of Gwydir Street, on the other side from the cemetery. As I familiarise myself with my new home town, I regularly take a walk past the coffee shop up the length of Gwydir Street. The terraced houses, many brand-new when Cousin Jessie lived there, hug the narrow pavement, externally not that much changed from their appearance in Victorian times. They have become newly fashionable, now that Mill Road is at the epicentre of twenty-first century hipster life.

It's also home to an active and knowledgeable community of local historians. One of them tells me that there has been much renumbering since the street was first built, so I can't be certain that the present No. 154 is the same house listed in the 1881 census as the home of Mrs Rooke and Jessie.

What is certain, though, is that their neighbours were working people in trades such as carpentry and joinery. There was a customs officer, builders and clerks. The head of the household at No.154 was one Ebenezer Canham, who described himself to the census taker as a cigar dealer. I find that this Dickensian-sounding character had previously been the publican of the Durham Ox, one of the many hostelries on Mill Road.

Ebenezer was a widower living with an adult son, called Henry who worked as a carpenter. No doubt he needed Mrs Rooke to cook and wash and clean for them both. As he was a similar age to Harriet, also known more familiarly as Hattie, I have to consider the possibility that the term 'housekeeper' provided cover for a more intimate relationship.

I look again at that studio photograph and decide that although the camera can lie, I could not believe that this epitome of respectability shared Ebenezer's bed. Surely it was more likely that she shared her bed with the infant girl. Neither the current No.154 Gwydir Street, nor the other two-storied terraced properties nearby looked as if they had the space to afford much privacy for the housekeeper and her young charge. This testosterone-filled house would surely have been a strange place for the toddler Jessie to grow up in.

Ebenezer Canham, whether kindly to her or not, clearly did not pretend he was her father; the census entry he made put her firmly in her place.

'Jessie A. Heading, 4, illegitimate.'

'Illegitimate' was all it said, in beautiful copper-plate handwriting. That was the whole description of this innocent four-year-old, not yet at school.

'Illegitimate'. It's a word that hammers itself into me, as I sit in the silence of the library reading the census entry.

I reach for a dictionary and hope to read a kinder twenty-first-century definition of the word that labelled Cousin Jessie, and could have done me. According to *Webster's Dictionary*:

> 'Illegitimate: not recognised as lawful offspring; not rightly deduced or inferred; departing from the regular; not sanctioned by law.'

while the *Oxford English Dictionary* puts it this way:

> 'Illegitimate: not authorised by the law; not in accordance with accepted standards or rules; born of parents not lawfully married to each other.'

So not much kindness there. My dad, who had also briefly been a publican, might well have had more difficulty than Ebenezer in making a full declaration to the census taker.

I have never thought of this before, but as the 1961 Census may not be published until 2062, I have to reconcile myself to never finding out just what Dad had declared about me and my mum. I wonder if my dad sought assurance from the official that the record would not be open to prying eyes – even his own daughter's – for a hundred years.

As for Jessie A. Heading, illegitimate, maybe Ebenezer wanted to distance himself from this child on the record and clearly Mrs Rooke did not pretend she was her own lawful child. Perhaps she explained to Ebenezer the nature of the arrangement she had made, and no doubt the extra income made it easier for him to accept another man's child into his household. There would have been no need for Mrs Rooke to give any more in the way of explanation – except perhaps to make it clear that this little girl had at least not been born in the workhouse.

I try to find Jessie's school record but meet the first real failure in my detective quest. She was certainly entitled to some elementary schooling, as she was in the first generation that benefited from the two Acts of Parliament of 1872 and 1880, which established public, that is, state schools, and required parents to ensure their children attended. Maybe Jessie attended St Matthew's, which is still going strong and lies close to Gwydir Street. A primary school education was the best Jessie could have hoped for; education was compulsory only to the age of ten.

Five years' schooling was deemed enough for girls like Jessie to master her three Rs, the basics of reading, writing and 'rithmetic – quite enough that is for a life of domestic service.

Leicester, 1963

Everything – and nothing – is about to change, and I don't quite realise it yet. What I do know is that this summer is a rite of passage, as I move up to big school.

I am one of only two girls in my primary school who has passed the eleven-plus – most of my class were not even entered for the exam. I am the only one who is going on to Wyggeston Girls' Grammar School.

Just passing the exam is not enough to get in there, though. Leicester City Council Education Committee operates a super-selective system, with the two Wyggeston schools, the Boys' and the Girls', considered the best of the six grammar schools in the city.

So, Mummy and Daddy show a rare pleasure, maybe give a little cheer, as they open the envelope with the good news that I have won a place. They proudly show me the typewritten letter before putting it carefully away in the sideboard drawer in our living room. Everything precious goes in there, as we do not have the luxury of a study, nor even space for a desk.

I don't remember any fond farewells with my classmates on leaving day. I never saw or heard from any of them ever again. I am happy and excited to move on. What became of Cherry with the flowing locks and her single parent, I will never know.

This summer holiday was where the excitement started. For one thing, there are several trips to the shops to buy the new school uniform and all the other items on a very long list.

The basic winter outfit is just the start: a dark skirt with a bib, two white, open-necked blouses but no tie, a gabardine mac, a velour hat, dark gloves, plus two pairs of shoes, indoor and out. Then there is the gym kit, including thick navy-blue knickers, which will soon come to epitomise my horror of PE lessons. A skirt and an Aertex shirt for games, plimsolls and hockey boots.

The list goes on: two overalls, one blue for Science, one white for a mysterious lesson called Housecraft. Then there is a new leather satchel and a pencil case to put into it, a geometry set, crayons for art, two dictionaries, English and French... on and on it goes. I have never been given so many new things all at once, and it never crosses my mind that my mother might have to go without to pay for it.

My parents do somehow manage to afford a summer holiday. Since last year, we have broken away from the routine of the boarding house in Bridlington, and now for me there is the excitement of visiting new places by the sea.

Last year, we went to a small resort called Cliftonville near Margate. That had involved a long drive at night through London in my dad's Ford Popular; he had not risked driving through the capital during the day. I sensed he was afraid of getting lost and was rattled by the traffic. This year, Clacton-on-Sea in Essex is our chosen destination, a safer choice as it could be reached cross-country from Leicester.

Maybe if I had known what was coming soon, I would have spotted something worrying in my mother's expression in the photographs from the seaside trip this year. An older and wiser observer might have noticed something forced about the smile for the camera, something ill at ease about this forty-seven-year-old woman, despite the sunshine at what should have been the most relaxed time of the year.

As for me, those photos show me still very much the child, with the same short, boyish hairdo that I have had since I was five. There is, however, more of a conscious pose for the camera and an obvious confidence in my demeanour. That's no doubt in part the product of seven years of private education, especially those elocution lessons. I have already changed a lot from that introverted infant who had started school with a speech defect.

On the last night of the holiday, there is a final treat. We go to the Pavilion to see the Clifford Henry Show. Children are invited on stage for a competition.

Of course, I rush to go up. The challenge is to do the Twist, the dance that has been all the rage since Chubby Checker's record made the hit parade last year. I had seen the dance on our black and white television and had learnt the moves from the screen.

To my amazement, I win first prize and Clifford Henry himself presents me with a certificate. I still have it, but sadly there is no photographic record of us all that evening, so I have nothing to show whether this little triumph cheered my mother up. I hope so.

My term begins immediately on our return home. The first few weeks of school pass uneventfully and I settle into a new routine.

My father drives me there, and picks me up. It fits in with his shifts at the Working Men's Club, where he works till three and then again after tea. I am still not trusted to go on the bus or enjoy the company of my new schoolmates out of class.

For the first time, I have homework to do every evening and at weekends, but I don't mind a bit as it gives me something to do in the long hours when I am by myself at home. I enjoy all my new subjects at school – well, the academic ones, that is.

I am not so keen on Art or on Housecraft, which turns out to be about sewing and cooking. The worst trial is PE. The gym contains instruments of torture: the horse, the ropes, the beam, the polished wooden climbing frames girding the walls, I dread them all. I am not tall enough for netball and do not run fast enough for hockey. I make a quiet resolution to lose weight to survive the thrice-weekly humiliation.

Then, after half-term, as the autumn draws on, the world darkens. The warning signs were there, although I am too young to read them.

My mother takes to her bed a lot, sometimes still being there when I come home from school. Daddy, as ever, says little but simply gets on with the business of keeping our household ticking over when he isn't at work, doing shopping and cleaning and occasionally making our tea. His signature dish is fried eggs and bacon.

Mummy's mysterious illness brings a bonus for me. At last I get a taste of some freedom.

My father still gives me a lift to school in the morning but I am sometimes allowed to catch the bus home on my own. I cheerfully bear the burden of carrying my smart new satchel, bulging with books needed for homework.

I am met off the bus, but what interesting possibilities are opened up by travelling without a parent on the No. 39! For one thing, I get to know the only one of my classmates who takes the same route. It seems that this bus does not go through parts of the city where many grammar school children live.

This new friendship with Ann, who lives over her parents'

shop, quite close to my house, is not, however, encouraged by Mummy. I get to visit the shop – but there will not be a return invitation to mine.

Once home, I change out of my school uniform, have my tea, Daddy goes back to work and I dutifully set to at the living room table, to do my homework. The TV is usually on in the corner, but I have quickly learned not to be distracted by it – except for one night in late November.

Friday night is History, and so I am studying a picture of a Babylonian ziggurat in my textbook about Ancient Civilisations when the newsflash comes on around seven thirty. A solemn newsreader tells me of the death of the young president in Dallas.

Maybe my mother is upstairs or is in the kitchen washing the tea things, so I am alone. My pen is frozen and I feel the shock that reverberates around the world. In that brutal instant, I learn that heroes are all too mortal and something of childish innocence falls away from me for good.

Then, not long after that, following a cheerless Christmas and with the new term begun, Daddy picks me up unexpectedly from school and tells me that Mummy has gone into hospital. He says little about what's wrong with her or why she is so ill that she has to stay there.

Maybe he is in shock, but I can't remember any hugs or words of comfort either – it isn't his style. I am told to say nothing at school about where my mother has been admitted, that she is in the Towers.

This forbidding-looking Victorian Gothic pile lies behind a long wall and a thick screen of trees only half a mile or so from where we live and close to Ann's shop. The Towers, I know somehow even at my age, perhaps from Ann, is not a hospital like the Infirmary or the General, the hospitals for physical illnesses.

No, this place is different, a place to be described, if at all, in whispers. It is Leicester's mental hospital, a place that some people still call the lunatic asylum.

We go there to visit the following evening. The darkness augments the air of menace from the tall red-brick towers over the façade and great stone entrance.

I feel anxious, fearful – of what, exactly? Do I imagine a Mrs Rochester figure will come screaming down the corridor, eyes ablaze with murderous intent?

I have a picture-book version of *Jane Eyre* and the image of the madwoman in the attic gripped my imagination and formed the basis of my understanding of what a woman with mental illness might be like.

Once inside, the cloud of fear soon dissipates. It is a perfectly ordinary place. Somewhat austere, yes, but it's not so different from the interior of my school, with walls painted in that familiar institutional pale-green colour, and also, like school, with long corridors, tiled on the walls. The floors are covered in a similar sludge-coloured linoleum to soften the sound of footsteps.

I am so relieved to see my mother on the ward, looking no different to how she was when I last saw her. She is in bed but sitting up and she smiles to see us. She says the doctor has said that she is 'so very, very tired' and that all she needs is rest. She implies – with apparent conviction – that it is the bad bout of flu she had at Christmas that was the cause of her collapse.

I suppose I say something cheering about my school day and Daddy asks practical questions about what Mummy needs him to bring in tomorrow, then we go home. I leave with a warm feeling that she is OK, that the nurses and doctors are kind, and that asylum means a place of peace and safety.

My mum comes home after a week or so and she seems to be better. Life resumes its normal groove.

Mummy stays at home, Daddy works long hours at the club and I continue my generally happy life at school. After my brief days of freedom of coming home on the bus, I am picked up from school in the car again.

There is no discussion, at least within reach of my ears, of how Mummy's well-being might be improved. The only hint I get is when my old Aunt Lizzie, a rare visitor to our household, comes around to offer her a herbal tonic to deal with what she calls her 'nerves'.

It is a very long time indeed before I understand any more. Still, for sure, another chunk of childishness has fallen away.

Cambridge, 2016

I am sure Jessie had to grow up quickly. There were few certainties or securities in most Victorian lives, and so it was on Gwydir Street.

My instinct about Mrs Rooke's respectability is confirmed when I discover that by the end of 1881 Ebenezer had remarried. A few years later, he was dead and buried in Mill Road Cemetery. Mrs Rooke may have stayed on to minister to his son Henry, I can't discover, but by the time Jessie was ten, they had certainly moved on.

I find Harriet in an 1887 Cambridge street directory living in lodgings in a long-demolished place called Vicar's Buildings. This was in a densely packed area of Victorian humanity with the market at its hub; now their little home lies under a shopping arcade.

Their neighbours were mainly women and children like themselves, including a few in the dressmaking and tailoring trade. Hattie and Jessie were living here, I realise, at the time that their formal studio portrait was taken.

Looking at it again, I am struck by the pride of bearing in both of them. Who is this stance for, I wonder?

Not just the photographer, that's for sure. For a Bedfordshire farmer, perhaps?

I take in all the details. The studio itself is dressed with a potted fern and a chintz drape. Mrs Rooke is seated, with the Bible in her hands. These appear unadorned with rings or bracelets – working hands. The Holy Book is no doubt a regular studio prop, helping keep the hands still, as well as heavily symbolic of Victorian respectability.

Harriet, now well into her fifties, looks younger than her years. She still has a pretty face, with her clear, light-coloured eyes counteracting her rather severe expression and rigid, slightly downturned mouth.

Her figure appears more matronly, with a full bust and waist, no doubt kept firmly pinched by the stays beneath. Her formal, full-length dress is, I think, in the late Victorian style, in a plain dark material, with a high neck, buttons and piping up the front and on the cuffs. A small oval brooch at the throat is her only jewellery.

Then to her left stands Jessie, her right arm on an unseen chair. She wears a dress that appears to be cut from the same cloth, also full-length, with a row of buttons up the front. Instead of piping, there is a rather elaborate puff sleeve and cuff, with a white lace collar at the high neck.

She looks out at me with rather sad, dark eyes, her mouth set in as severe an expression as Mrs Rooke's. I note a rather long face, and straight, shoulder-length hair that appears to be of a light brown, what used to be called rather disparagingly a mousey colour. Although she has even features, it does not look as if she would ever become a beauty or even conventionally pretty – indeed Mrs Rooke has the prettier face.

Then it strikes me. By the age of thirteen, with her school days firmly behind her, Jessie may well no longer have even seen herself as a child. She is projecting herself in this photograph as an aspiring adult about to enter the world of work. It is a sort of coming-of-age picture.

This seems clear in the entry I find in the 1891 Census, taken just a year or so after this photo. Hattie, as head of their humble household, describes the now fourteen-year-old Jessie as a 'dressmaker's apprentice'. And the word 'illegitimate' is no longer there. Instead Jessie Heading is described as a 'boarder'.

Better a boarder than a bastard, I reckon. Still not proper family, though.

Chapter Three

Cambridge, 2016

A life in a small book: a Cambridge life, lost but treasured and now in my hands.

I am cradling a pocket-sized red leather-bound volume which I have taken from the box file. It is a pleasure to feel the warm soft covers between the palms. In the absence of any diaries or letters, it is almost the only thing I have containing Cousin Jessie's handwriting, so one of the most precious to me of all the objects in the box. I also realise that there are clues in here which may tell me more about the people she valued enough to keep their names and mark their significant dates.

The title page declares it to be '*a Birthday Book of Cheering and Consolatory Texts, selected from Scripture and other Sources.*' There is no publication date inside but I find via an antiquarian book website that it was published in 1883 and that there was only one edition.

There is no name on the flyleaf but I realise that it may have originally belonged to Mrs Rooke – it is not a childish object. One of the more faded entries within it is that of *Jessie A. Heading* written in a very careful script on her birthday of January 25, no doubt by her adoptive mother.

I note the A again: the Ashbowl of her father's family.

I set myself to go through every listing, cross-referencing

with the censuses, registers and street directories. It is quite a task.

Inside the birthday book it is set out like a diary, with three days on each right-hand page and on the left a daily quotation or homily from the Bible or other uplifting text. There are about thirty entries in all.

Some are in pencil, as if provisional – or maybe inserted by the young Jessie, unsure of her rights over the book. The majority are in permanent black ink. Those handful where the ink has faded to brown, I conclude were probably the earliest entries, maybe inscribed when the book was acquired, so in the years when Jessie was still a child.

As well as Jessie's name, that of Daisy Fromant is among that small number inscribed meticulously by Mrs Rooke. Fromant, I know, was her maiden name, so Daisy was family, probably her niece and a near contemporary of Cousin Jessie.

I find Daisy listed in the 1891 census as a domestic servant, aged just thirteen, working on a country estate close to Newmarket. Ten years later, she has moved to Cambridge, to Bridge Street, a short walk from her aunt and sort-of-cousin.

By the time of that 1901 census, Hattie and Jessie had moved again, this time to Silver Street, where Mrs Rooke became housekeeper to a dentist. Now Jessie is claimed by Hattie as her '*adopted daughter*': no longer illegitimate, no longer a boarder, claimed as kin at last.

I realise that there was no formal adoption available in law for another generation but it was something real nevertheless. At an age when Jessie was free to move out from the housekeeper's embrace, free to marry, free to take domestic service under another roof, she was still, at the age of twenty-four, tied to the generous apron strings of this Victorian matron.

The first entry in permanent black ink, indeed the very first in the book, is that of one Kate Muncey, listed on January 16. She too, I discover, is related to Mrs Rooke, as her sister married into the large Muncey family. So complex a clan it is that it is hard to work out who is related to whom but Kate I conclude is probably also Hattie's niece.

I learn that she is nearly a decade younger than Jessie, first finding her as a five-year-old child in the 1891 census. By 1901 she too is a domestic servant aged fifteen and working in a big house outside Cambridge, called Milton Hall.

Later in January comes the first of several entries marking the births of babies in the early years of the twentieth century. Might they be the same ones whose photographs Jessie took with her to Canada, I wonder?

I take those photos out of their envelope again. The smiling infants and toddlers posed for the photographer in Cambridge studios, in their spotless white gowns, are all anonymous.

Why keep those pictures, take them thousands of miles across the ocean and keep them for more than half a century after that unless they had meaning for Jessie? The fourteen-year-old dressmaker's apprentice became the twenty-something children's nurse – a nanny in modern parlance. These pictures were of her 'children', her lost 'children', weren't they? I return the photographs to the envelope and mull over just what Jessie lost when she left England.

There is tragedy inscribed in the little red book too. In a March entry I find another young servant woman called

Mabel Porter.

I trace her not only in the birth registers but also in the deaths; she died at the age of just seventeen in 1900. Life was a fragile thing then, of course. Infectious diseases like flu, TB and diphtheria took the young as well as the old with endemic suffering, pain and loss, assuaged by the comforts of the Christian faith.

As I go through the months, I pause sometimes to read the homilies, some familiar from hymns, psalms and sermons.

'In my Father's house are many rooms'... 'Come unto me, all ye that labour and are heavy laden and I will give you rest'... 'The Lord is my shepherd, no want I shall know'... 'I will lift up mine eyes unto the hills from whence cometh my help. My help cometh from the Lord'... 'Our God, our help in ages past, Our hope for years to come' and particularly pertinent for the lives of Daisy, Kate, Mabel and Jessie the May 5 entry: 'A servant with this clause makes drudgery divine: who sweeps a room as for thy laws, makes that and the action fine.'

As I continue through the Spring, Summer and into the Autumn of this godly calendar, I am struck by something. Nearly all the names are female.

The first male name I come across is not till late August, that of Thomas Drake. He was born in 1894, so was likely to have been one of Jessie's young charges. The Harold Drake a few pages on is his younger brother.

The Drake family command half a dozen entries between them. I find them in an old street directory running the Cavendish Stores on the Hills Road, living over the shop. Edith Drake, the boys' older sister, is described as a dressmaker in the 1901 census; perhaps Jessie had come across her from her time in Vicar's buildings when she served as an apprentice in that trade. Maybe Jessie helped Edith out with the sewing or looked after the younger children, while their parents and the eldest daughter served out front.

I reach December and still find no male contemporaries of Cousin Jessie's. There are no Headings nor McDonalds either – so the only family Jessie might have claimed apart from Mrs Rooke would have been her two nieces, Kate and Daisy.

There were clearly enough young women between these covers to provide company, especially during the long working day. There were also babies a-plenty to rock to sleep, feed, wash, and clean up after but I can find no sign at all that Jessie ever found a sweetheart, let alone a husband.

Many people, certainly at that time, might regard that as the hole in her Cambridge life but they'd call it a godly life. It was a settled one, modest and hard-working for sure but not one obviously from which Jessie needed to escape – and at least she had friends.

Leicester, 1964

Mummy is making some crusty cheese and onion cobs and I am watching. It is a new venture to provide some outdoor catering for the club.

First, she halves the cobs – or bread rolls as you might call them. Then she butters them generously. She has grated a large mound of red Leicester cheese in a bowl and takes a handful, again a generous one and packs it onto the bottom half of the cob. Then come slices of raw onion, two or three per cob. Finally, she presses the hard-baked caramelised top of the bun down firmly on the base.

She will then place it into the large tray in which the baker supplied the cobs. After an hour or so, the tray is full.

Mummy doesn't take them round to the club. Daddy collects them in time for that day's customers to have with their pint.

I offer to help. I am twelve now after all. Mummy thinks about it and says I can butter the cobs; she doesn't want to risk my cutting myself grating or slicing. We get into a rhythm together – a mini production-line.

There's good news from Daddy. They sell 'like hot cakes' he says.

We make more – two bakers' trays – but Mummy and I soon exhaust our capacity to increase production. Then it all stops.

After just a few weeks, Daddy does the sums and realises there is no profit in it at the price people are prepared to pay. The enterprise comes to an end as soon as it began.

He may have been disappointed that it did not bring in some extra income, but I thought it was worthwhile as it was clearly cheering Mummy up. It may well have been a therapeutic venture but if there was no profit in it, then it had to end.

I always had school to fall back on but Mummy…well, I suppose I was her only friend as well as her daughter. We talked a lot, Mummy sitting in her armchair and I, sitting close by on the sofa or sometimes on the rug in front of her chair.

She'd talk sometimes about her life in the years before the war – about her girlfriends. There was a Dorothy, a Phyliss and a Joan, but they seemed to have disappeared from her post-war life. She didn't tell me why.

She also told me about a boyfriend or two before Daddy – one, a dashing RAF man. She clearly had known fun and parties and dancing but it had all gone now.

Looking back now, though, I think there was a certain frustration in her life before the war. She left school at fourteen, elementary school they called it then, in the summer of 1930. She got good marks, especially for English, but that was the end of schooling for her, even though some of her brothers and sisters stayed on another couple of years. She told me proudly that Daddy had gone to a grammar school but had to leave at sixteen to go to work.

Mummy learnt shorthand typing but I don't think office work satisfied her very much. It was just a job.

Outside work, she'd become interested in what was called the Nature Cure movement and became a vegetarian. That was unusual then – setting you apart from the norm. Mummy was influenced by one of her older brothers who was not only a vegetarian but a pacifist, which in the 1930s put you really beyond the pale.

She told me she enjoyed poetry as her brother Ken did too but she had just the one book of poems, an anthology, which she kept in a drawer. The only bookshelves in our house were in my bedroom.

We didn't get visitors at home of course, but if we had they would have found it a dull sort of place, I suppose. If you'd got over the threshold, you would not have been asked into the front room, which others might have kept in pristine shape as a best parlour. That was because no fire was ever set in the grate there, and there was little in the way of furnishings – apart from an upright piano.

I have no idea where that came from. Maybe it was already in the house when we'd moved in. Perhaps an old piano had been brought here from the upstairs room at the club, replaced there by a newer model. It was the only reason I ever found to go in there: childishly testing the keys but easily dismayed by the discordant noise I produced. That frustration – plus the cold – drove me back to the living room next door before long.

The fire blazes in the hearth all day long from the 1st of November until May in there. Daddy, always the first to rise, made sure there was enough coal in the basket by the grate to keep it going through the day.

Mummy would rake it to remove the ashes and throw a hunk or two of coal onto the fire to rekindle it. She always feels the cold and often stands directly in front of the flames, lifting her skirt a little to warm the back of her legs.

This room unlike the one next door is packed with furniture. In front of the fire is the three-piece suite: the small sofa which I usually sit on and the two armchairs, one for Mummy and one for Daddy.

Beyond the fireplace towards the window stands our television, the screen framed in dark wood, on a metal stand with a shelf on which sits the Radio Times. Then in front of the window stands the large wooden cabinet, containing what we call the wireless and a record turntable. The record collection is in there too: a handful of 78s which are Daddy's, plus my two Beatles LPs and a small but growing number of 45s.

Then hard against the back of the sofa stands the dining table with just three chairs. The fourth chair stands unused against the fourth wall which is dominated by the sideboard. There's just room on the floor in the corner between the sideboard and the dining table for a sewing machine in its dark wooden case and close by it, Mummy's knitting bag.

She'd made me a striped blue jumper which turned out well although I feared it made me look fat. She'd also got something for Daddy on the go now. It is something, I suppose, to replace the abandoned catering enterprise.

Beyond the living room, is a small kitchen and pantry. Sometimes Mummy and I make a cake together in there, usually a Victoria sponge. I like the raw cake mixture best, scraped from the wooden spoon.

I don't think Mummy gets much pleasure from cooking. She tells me how her mother – the grandmother I never knew – shopped in the market to buy the cheapest cuts of meat and then served up nutritious meals on a small budget for her father – the grandfather McDonald I also never knew – and up to ten children at a sitting.

My mouth puckered in mock distaste as Mummy described the tripe and onions, the bread and dripping and the other bilious-sounding dishes, which she declared to be delicious. She preferred those days I am sure, when there were lots of people around the dining table and noise and bustle always around the house.

She tells me of how much she loved Christmas then, with

a party in the McDonald home on Boxing Day every year. Christmases weren't like that now, that's for sure.

It would always be just the three of us for Christmas dinner and usually on Boxing Day as well. Daddy worked on Christmas morning so by the late afternoon after the turkey and the pudding, as we sat by the telly, Daddy was usually the first to doze off.

As the grey light faded, I did not dare put the light on. I could neither read nor put a record on the turntable. It was too cold upstairs to retreat to my bedroom, so I was stuck, until Mummy or Daddy woke up and got up to get the tea.

At least the house looked cheerier at Christmas. We had a little plastic tree with baubles and tinsel placed on the sideboard. There were hand-made paper streamers, red, green, pink and blue looped on the walls and on the staircase.

At other times, the house seems reduced to its essential functionality; no love, time nor money were wasted on decoration or ornaments beyond the dull Dutch painting over the mantelpiece. I suppose it made it easier to keep the place clean. Mummy hated housework at the best of times and when she is ill, she does even less of it.

After all, it is not ours; it belongs to the Gipsy Lane Working Men's Club. Maybe Mummy plans on not staying here too long although we have been here more than five years already. A small portion of Mummy and Daddy's life for sure – it's nearly half my lifetime though.

Somehow, it's still not home and maybe it never will be.

Cambridge, 2016

I am walking around Jessie's Cambridge. I have shaken off that feeling of being a tourist or at best a temporary resident here. I am becoming more comfortable calling this city my home.

I stand in front of No.3 Silver Street, which even the curious tourist might miss on the walking route from King's College Chapel to the Mathematical Bridge. It is an imposing but anonymous flat-fronted, three-storied terraced building at the heart of historic Cambridge. The maroon-coloured door does not have a sign on it, neither is there a functioning doorbell or knocker. The barber's shop on the ground floor next door is the only face presented to the outside world along this terrace.

I eventually work out that the entrance to the house is from the rear, accessible only via St Catherine's College around the corner. It's now student accommodation, taken back for this purpose in 1947 after it ceased to be a dental practice.

Back in the first decades of the twentieth century, I expect it was hard and demanding work for Hattie, even if assisted by Jessie, to keep the place clean and in order for Mr Rhodes the dentist and his sons. I crane my eyes up to the windows on the third floor and wonder if Mrs Rooke and her adopted daughter had their rooms up there. I imagine them on a winter's evening, keeping warm by the fire in candle or gaslight.

I take another walk, this time up Bridge Street through the crowds walking towards the punt station by the River Cam and look out for the house where Daisy lived and where I believe Jessie worked for a while too. At least a couple of the babies recorded in the birthday book were born here when the street was a smart residential one, rather than the bustling hub for tourists and shoppers, with cafes, pubs, restaurants, shops and punt promoters competing for their custom along its length now.

On another expedition, I go in the other direction from the town centre, up the Hills Road to look for the site where the Drakes' shop was. As well as the dressmaking business and the general stores, there was a cycle repair shop there too, all run by the family. No doubt they enjoyed good trade from the County Boys' School next door, now a Sixth Form College.

Maybe Cousin Jessie had a cycle to get the two miles to the Drakes'. It was not seen as ladylike to cycle in the first decade of the twentieth century but then Jessie wasn't a lady, was she? Can I imagine her in her long skirt, peddling along the almost straight road from town and then puffing as she went up the long steep path over the railway bridge, then freewheeling down the other side?

I wonder too whether Jessie might have visited Kate Muncey at Milton Hall. It's five miles outside Cambridge, so I take a drive to find it.

The hall which is now a conference centre looks from the outside much as it would have done in 1900. I stop to admire the Georgian building, a former manor house with its grand pillared entrance and portico which once was at the centre of a large estate.

Might Cousin Jessie have taken tea with her sort-of-cousin

in the servants' quarters? Is this Jessie I see arriving in her Sunday-best, a little out of breath, crunching down the gravel drive?

Silver Street, Bridge Street, Hills Road, Milton Hall… until her thirtieth birthday in 1907, this was the length and breadth of Jessie's world, it seemed. Then something changed and she started on the path which led to that one-way steamship ride to Canada.

I am thinking that young Kate Muncey had a hand in it.

I have on my kitchen table another large brown envelope with a Canadian postmark. It is the first mail I have received from across the Atlantic since the correspondence with Mrs Jenkins at the Office of the Public Guardian nearly five years ago.

I have learnt that Cousin Jessie's immigration record might be a very helpful document and that it would be worthwhile paying the Canadian archive a few dollars to send me a full copy. I eagerly open the envelope.

What is inside surprises: it doesn't look like the copy of a shipping record as I was expecting. Rather it is a photocopy of a ledger entry of an application written, not at the port in Canada but at a desk in England.

Here she is: Jessie Heading, address given as 2 Benet Street, Cambridge, date of birth stated as January 25th, 1880.

1880! I knew well enough that Jessie was born three years earlier in 1877. Why this big little lie?

I read on.

Jessie is commended by a Miss Borrer of Cambridge to a Mrs Sillitoe of Vancouver and is to set sail for Canada on a ship called the Ionian on November 7, 1912.

There was a forwarding address too: a poste restante in a place called Burnaby, B.C, care of a Mrs Muncey – an unusual – as well as familiar – name for sure.

This wasn't my Kate Muncey though. I checked and re-checked and I am sure she never left England. It turns out to be Kate's sister-in-law Sarah who along with her husband William had emigrated to Canada just the year before.

Back in 1901 William, nearly twenty years older than Kate and nearly ten years older than Jessie lived and worked in Cambridge as a coal cart man, while Sarah worked at home, taking in laundry. They never featured in Jessie's birthday book but surely Jessie might have been acquainted with them. Maybe Kate told excited tales of their hopes and dreams for their new lives out in British Columbia.

I think I have a photograph of Kate. I take it out of the box.

It is a very striking studio portrait of a young woman in a lovely white cotton lawn blouse, in the Edwardian style, with a rose pinned to her bosom. She has thick dark hair upswept in a looser style than the late Victorians had favoured. She has a fuller face than Cousin Jessie's and bears a more confident expression. Kate is striking the pose of a modern young woman – a twentieth-century pose – so different from the modest demeanour of the nineteenth-century Jessie in her *carte de visite*.

The more recent portrait does not have any signature but bears the photographer's inscription – Portland Studios, Craven Park Road, Harlesden. I know that, at least in 1908, Kate was in North West London and that Cousin Jessie was in London too.

I take the card out of the box which proves it. It is a birthday card, still in its original envelope, the only one Jessie had kept and taken across the ocean with her. There is a drawing of violets on one side and handwritten greetings on the other. Postmarked Maida Hill, London NW and dated 24 January 1908, which was the eve of Jessie's thirty-first birthday, it was signed simply Kate.

The address on the envelope was hard to decipher but I finally make it out: 88, Overstrand Mansions, Battersea. I check this address on a property website and confirm that this was one of those grand Edwardian mansion blocks overlooking the park on Prince of Wales' Drive – very desirable now and then. I couldn't imagine that Jessie was visiting such an address. It was much more likely that she was working there.

So the twenty-two-year old Kate and the thirty-one-year old Jessie were in London at the same time. Did the younger woman take the first step away from the confines of Milton Hall?

There is no way of telling. I just have an instinct that Kate might have taken the initiative and might have persuaded her older sort-of-cousin to go to London too.

I need to find out more about Jessie's time in the capital, short though I think it may have been. It may well have been the first time she'd taken a train, I realise. Perhaps Kate went with her.

I see them waved off from Cambridge station by a tearful Daisy waving her white handkerchief and by the more restrained Hattie, who may have disapproved of the whole venture. I imagine the two women arriving into the splendour and noise of the Victorian railway terminus at Liverpool Street. Maybe they embraced as they said goodbye – the one heading for Maida Vale, the other across the river to Battersea.

I go down to London to spend a day in the South London archives to try to find out more about Jessie's time there. I delve into street directories, voters' lists, Post Office files and the rest but fail to find any record of Jessie anywhere.

All I can find are the names of the householders in Overstrand Mansions. Living at No.88 in 1907 there was a Mr Cyril L. Longhurst. By the time of the 1911 Census he had moved to a house nearby and was listed as a civil servant with a wife and a three-year-old baby. So it could have been that the Longhursts hired a nanny around 1907 or 8 but I felt disappointed I had nothing more concrete to show for my day in the archives.

Until, that is, I get home and go back to the birthday book. There in November, is a L. Longhurst. I check and I can find no baby Longhurst born in Cambridge around that time. This is the confirmation I need that Jessie had indeed worked in London.

She didn't stay there long though, maybe just the one year nursing the Longhurst baby, three years at most. By the time of the 1911 Census Cousin Jessie is back in the Cambridge area.

It has taken me a while to track her down in this record, unlike those of the earlier censuses, when she was living with Mrs Rooke. I have become cannier with my online searches. Sometimes, I have learned, it is better to input less information in the search box than you actually know.

So having drawn a blank, when I put in Jessie's date of birth as 1877 and her first name as Jessie, I resubmit the inquiry. I input the date of birth as plus or minus five years of 1877 and put simply the initial J in the first name box. This cracks it.

I find a Jenie Heading stated as aged thirty living as a children's nurse in a doctor's household in a village outside Cambridge. I know immediately that it is my Jessie because of the distinctive middle name of Ashbowl.

Had Dr Ackroyd just guessed at her age when completing the census form, I wonder? Or was it the first time that the now thirty-four-year old woman claimed to be rather younger than her real age? – as she did again in the immigration record the following year.

Maybe Jessie had returned to Cambridge earlier, in time for Daisy's marriage in August 1908 to a Mr Percy Blunt. The ceremony took place in Grantchester Church.

It is hard now to imagine the scene before its famous War Memorial was erected – the one with the poet Rupert Brooke's name among those inscribed on it. 'Stands the clock at ten to three…is there honey still for tea?' That poem in celebration of the lost idyll of pre-First World War England comes to me now as I walk past it, enter the porch and stand in the quiet of the nave.

Yes, I think I see Cousin Jessie sitting in the pews on the bride's side of the aisle. Perhaps Kate Muncey was bridesmaid.

I see Jessie again as she stands outside the church watching as the bride throws her bouquet. It is Kate who catches it, becoming Mrs Gilson just a few years later.

No doubt Jessie wished them both every happiness but she could be forgiven for also feeling a little sad. Now very much the spinster, what life stretched ahead of her?

Maybe, rather than Daisy's wedding, it was Mrs Rooke's increasing infirmity that brought her adoptive daughter back from her London adventure. Hattie was still in Silver Street, still a working housekeeper but less than a year after the census recorded her daughter back in service near Cambridge, Mrs Rooke went to her final rest.

She died in Addenbrooke's hospital on April 17, 1912. The hospital superintendent declared that she died of a heart condition at the age of seventy-eight. Just months later, Jessie left England for good.

Before she packed her bags, I see her, perhaps assisted by Daisy, performing the grim task of clearing out Hattie's earthly goods from the rooms in Silver Street. No doubt a new housekeeper needed to be installed. Jessie, it seems, didn't want the job.

Surely Daisy and she might have paused from time to time as they went through Mrs Rooke's belongings, to mull over those things which would have brought back memories of their own childhoods. Jessie would have smiled surely to see again that solemn Victorian studio portrait of her with the only mother she had ever known.

What might have been said when they came across a black-framed card, announcing the death of a man called William Heading, nearly a decade before? Did Jessie show it to Daisy with a few words about her blood grandfather or sweep it up quickly, putting it in her bag, along with the studio portrait and the birthday book?

One of the questions that nags at me the most is just what did Jessie ever know about her origins? That memorial card apart – there is still no clue.

What, if anything, did Daisy know about how her friend and adoptive cousin came to live with her aunt? What story might Mrs Rooke have woven to explain Jessie's surname and the reason for her distinctive middle name of Ashbowl?

Had she ever found the right time to tell the truth, or some of it, to Jessie? Or had she kept her silence, perhaps telling Jessie that her natural mother was dead – a lie, of course, but an easy one cutting off further uncomfortable enquiries.

Three generations later, that habit of locking away family secrets was still engrained. Yes, I know that – for sure I know that.

It makes me think that Mrs Rooke might well have taken Mary Ann Heading's secret to her grave: a secret never to be told.

Chapter Four

Mid-Atlantic, September 2016

C anada here we come!

We are cruising at thirty-five thousand feet with the little screen in front of my seat indicating that our plane is arcing over the Atlantic about half-way towards our destination of Halifax, Nova Scotia. There's little turbulence and a smooth flight is promised.

I have taken an unexpected opportunity to go to Canada for the first time. My daughter is attending a conference in Nova Scotia and, knowing about my quest, has asked me if I want to accompany her on the trip.

Of course, I do. I jump at the chance.

Although Cousin Jessie didn't arrive at this port, but in Quebec, still, I know I will be getting closer to her here. She occupies an increasing proportion of my thoughts – and my imagination now. As we travel on our six-hour flight in comfort, used as we are now to what would have been a miraculous form of transport for Cousin Jessie's generation, I can't help but think about that more arduous and perilous journey she undertook one hundred years before.

I hope someone came to wave her off from the Port of London and shed a tear for her as she began her one-way journey. I see her striding up the gangplank with porters sparing her the strain of carrying her own suitcase. I can never know if someone stood at the dockside as she boarded, whether Kate or Daisy, but if not, then at least, surely, it would have been easier not to look back.

Now she is at sea and I spot her in the crowd – a woman standing alone at a steamship rail testing the morning air.

I shiver: it is distinctly colder today.

The woman is pulling a cloak more tightly around her shoulders.

Cousin Jessie, for surely it is she, even though her back is turned towards me, seems to be craning her neck to look at the wheeling seagulls overhead. They look so effortlessly free, so careless of the grey, grey heaving ocean beneath them.

Is Jessie uplifted by the scene or made anxious, as I am, by the boundless and ungovernable waves all around us? She will know, as I do, that seven days into her journey she has gone well past the point of no return.

I don't believe she had ever been to sea before, not even on a seaside pleasure boat. Likely, she'd done nothing more on the water than be borne along the Cam on one of those wooden punts that Jack Scudamore had started hiring out in Cambridge on summer afternoons a few years before.

She had little experience to prepare her for what might be the ordeal of her life; the first trial being the autumnal weather and the increasing risk of storms as the journey progressed. Not the only trial though – perhaps Daisy or the more worldly-wise Kate had given Jessie some warnings – and not just about seasickness.

There would have been all sorts of conditions of people, men, women and children on board, including passengers from France and other European countries. They had been picked up by the Ionian from the port of Le Havre, its first stop, before it headed westwards across the Atlantic.

Perhaps her friends would have instilled suspicion into Jessie of these foreigners; warning her of the risks of getting too close to people, of pickpockets, contagion from disease, even the risk of giving too much away in idle chat.

She would have discovered too that even those she might see as God-fearing young women like herself would share her journey only as far as Quebec and then would scatter to a string of destinations around their vast new country. It might have seemed pointless to Jessie to invest too much time or energy in getting to know them.

I fear she is still alone.

As I see her now, her cloaked head facing the wind, I hope she takes comfort, even inspiration, from the wild beauty of the ocean, rather than being overwhelmed with fear. Jessie knew all too well the story of the most modern and luxurious ship in the world, the Titanic, and its fateful encounter with an iceberg, just seven months before.

Maybe she took some consolation from her birthday book homilies and prayers to keep these elemental powers at bay on her journey. I must encourage her in my own way, too.

I want to call out 'It will be alright, Jessie, I know you will get safely to Quebec'.

No voice comes out from me or it is drowned out by the wind. I run towards her but she is out of reach.

Jessie is gone. I wake up.

Halifax, Nova Scotia, 2016

Put your seat belts on, landing is in thirty minutes. The cabin announcement stirs me from my fitful sleep.

After our short flight over the northern curve of the earth, electronic visas speed our arrival through the airport and by the cocktail hour we are on the rooftop terrace of our hotel taking in our first sight of Halifax. What a view!

The great harbour in all its majesty is spread out before us. A century before this sight had offered hope and relief to millions of immigrants and sailors. Our gaze focusses on an old-fashioned sailing ship moored close to the waterfront: it's just for the tourists now, we suppose.

My daughter has a spare day before the start of the conference so we decide to visit together the immigration museum. It is called Pier 21 after the landing point for those setting foot on Canadian soil here.

It is a historic place but with a contemporary purpose, offering a positive view of immigration as at the heart of the Canadian story. It is a salutary experience for us, coming as it does just a few months after the shock of the Brexit referendum result and the refugee crisis on Southern European shores which preceded it.

We decide to take the tour. Our guide asks the members of the tour party who has family who emigrated here – perhaps after the Second World War, she suggests. Several people put their hands up.

Do I put mine up too? Cousin Jessie is family now to me, isn't she? I decide not to but just on a technicality, because it was not here that Jessie landed.

As we walk around the spacious floors, an uplifting ambience seems to wrap itself around us. Perhaps inevitably Pier 21's portraiture of the immigration experience in the nineteenth and early twentieth centuries is on the rosy side.

For one thing, as it is focussed on those arriving by sea, there is little reference to the many arrivals who I have learnt came over the land border from the United States. Among them were many enslaved people of colour and other fugitives from the American law man, who were not so well-received.

The fact was that some immigrants were deemed more desirable than others. Fortunately for Jessie, white, working class Englishwomen were on the desirable side of the tally. Since the 1870s, domestic servants, overwhelmingly female, were deemed 'preferred' occupations, along with farming families.

Jessie's timing was also fortunate: the early twentieth century was a period of huge expansion in Canada, especially in the West. Jessie was one of a million or so British immigrants who arrived in the decade before the First World War.

One of the exhibits catches my attention. It is an advertising poster, published around 1910 by a Canadian government agent based in the City of London, and which proclaimed its offer of:

'Assisted passages to Farm Labourers and Female Domestic Servants by the Magnificent Steam ships of the Allan Royal Mail Line'.

Highlighted in red is its offer of 'Free Grants of Land,

Good Wages, Cheap Provisions, Light taxes, Free Schools.'

How alluring a prospect that would have sounded for someone like Cousin Jessie!

We arrive now at the mock-up of the Canadian Pacific Railway's so-called 'colonist trains' and accept the tour guide's invitation to sit in a carriage and view the projected image of mountain scenery from the window. How marvellous that first sight of the Rockies would have been to Jessie, used as she was to the flatlands of East Anglia!

How daunting too those towering snowy peaks might have been. It would not have taken her much time on this journey to confirm that she really was in a foreign country, as her train wended its slow way through thousands of miles of vast still only partly-tamed wilderness.

That cross-continental journey by the steam trains of the Canadian Pacific Railway took immigrants like Jessie a full week more after their long sea journey. This was not a picture postcard tourist ride; it was surely a journey into the unknown.

Our guide – ever seeing the brighter side of the immigrants' experience – also points out to us a small cooker, a hob and a small oven, which she tells us was provided at the end of each railway carriage for the passengers to make coffee or cook a hot meal. You could buy provisions at a stall in the immigration hall, the prices usefully set out in foreign currency as well as the Canadian dollar. Maybe Jessie bought herself a few tins and packets and maybe she took her turn to make a frugal hot meal. Still it was no picnic for sure.

Moving on, we are invited to stop now at the battered

children's trunks spread around the hall, placed there to remind us that many small children braved the long journeys with precious few possessions and some of them in a pretty vulnerable state. Cousin Jessie, I realise, was indeed, relatively speaking, amongst the more privileged arrivals.

One of the black and white photographs on display in particular brings this home to me. It is captioned:

'Yanaluk family: Slavic immigrants arrive at the Port of Quebec c1911.'

There on a boardwalk staring calmly but in the case of at least two of the three small children, apprehensively, were this pathetic family group: father, mother with a small child peeping out from a cloak swathed around her back, and two small girls, neither older than seven.

After the tour, I go alone to the research room, to see what might be held there about the arrival of my immigrant cousin into the Port of Quebec in the following year. The librarian takes little time to find what I am looking for.

Would I like a full copy for a modest charge? Of course, I would.

I have already seen the entry online, taken from the *Passenger Lists 1865–1935* database, in the digitised Canadian archive, but the much-magnified photocopy that is soon presented to me shows more detail than I had seen before.

Here is the full extract from this passenger record of the Ionian steamship which arrived in Quebec on the 18th November 1912. I read the handwritten entry carefully across the columns from left to right:

'Passenger No 4... No of Steamship ticket 04899...
Amount of Cash in $25.
Name Heading Jessie... Female Age 30... Single...
British Bonus Allowed
Country of Birth England Race of People English
Destination New Westminster B.C.
Previous Occupation: Domestic... Intended occupation:
Domestic
Religious Denomination: C of E... Travel inland on:
CPR.'

Alongside Jessie on the same page, were listed twenty of her fellow passengers in Second Class. They came from every part of the United Kingdom: Scotland, Ireland, Wales as well as England. Others came from France, where the Ionian had made its first stop. The youngest listed here was six years old and the oldest forty. Their Canadian destinations – Ontario, Montreal, Alberta, Winnipeg – suggested that Jessie was the only one, at least in this group, going to British Columbia.

Some came with as little as $5 in their pockets. That was the minimum savings you had to have to be allowed entry, apparently. Again, Jessie with her $25 worth was relatively well-off.

Well, yes, relatively. It seemed she had been careful with her money, maybe putting a little bit aside, week by week over the past twenty years since she had started work.

The range of her fellow-travellers' occupations surprises me: there's a fifteen-year-old dairymaid planning to take up domestic service in her new country; a twenty-nine-year old bookkeeper coming to Canada to marry – intended occupation, housewife; the oldest of the group, a forty-year-old Roman Catholic woman declared herself to be a journalist. There was a solicitor, an engraver, a baker, a couple of clerks, a cook and a waiter as well as a farmer and two more domestic servants.

Then the librarian hands me a single photocopied page, with a black and white photo of a single-funnelled, four-mast steamship: the Ionian. I read that she was a boat of the Allan Canadian Pacific line, built in Belfast in 1901 to ply the Atlantic. I learn that she was four hundred and seventy feet long, and could travel at a speed of 14 knots.

There were three decks, accommodating three hundred and twenty-five second class passengers and eight hundred in third class. The ship had been recently reconfigured to remove the First class cabins it seemed. Jessie again was fortunate to be travelling Second Class.

In the last sentence on the page comes a jolting shock: the Ionian had come to a sorry end fewer than five years after Jessie's journey. It was sunk by a German U boat in 1917. When the immigration trade was forced to stop two years after Jessie's crossing, the steamship was re-purposed for wartime service.

Armed with a clutch of printed-off sheets and the satisfaction that my trip here has already paid dividends within hours of our arrival, I walk out with my daughter into the bright early Autumn afternoon. The crystal-clear maritime light blinds us temporarily. Out in the harbour, a large and dazzling cruise ship sails towards its mooring.

We take a stroll along the promenade which tracks the length of the waterfront, by cafes, food and souvenir stalls. It feels now like a tourist town as much as a still-working port – and a rapidly changing one too. The red cranes towering over the container terminal are vying to breach the sky highest with the building cranes, which stand sentinel over the still compact town, dwarfing the old fort on the hill.

Its future may be very different, but it is Halifax's history that intrigues me more, especially the events of 1912. Tomorrow I will be returning to that time again.

The next morning finds me now alone – my daughter having taken herself off to the conference – in the lobby of the Maritime Museum of the Atlantic. Once again, the purest of lights floods the modern airy lobby.

There are small yachts on display near the ticket office, boats you can imagine cheerfully bobbing on the ocean. I know though that this is not going to be a cheerful visit.

At the desk, I am given a map of the museum and I am pointed to the rooms which might interest me. One of them records the huge explosion which devastated Halifax and killed thousands of its citizens in 1917, an event which somehow seems to have disappeared from my history books.

Then there is a room where I can see exhibits from the Second World War, when Halifax harbour was of huge strategic significance and when the Atlantic convoys sought shelter here, stopping to take on fresh cargoes after their perilous journeys under fire. I have an uncle who is in his late nineties now and who served on those, so I will visit that room for him.

Yet there is one room that is the most compelling. I go there first, drawn just by the magnetic spell of its name. I pass swiftly through the hall with its models of other steam boats like the Franconia until I stop at the one marked with the boldest of capital letters TITANIC.

It would have dwarfed the Ionian and was famously considered the most advanced liner of its kind at the time. Also built in a Belfast shipyard, it had just two masts but four funnels – that in sheer power was progress. Its top speed was some twenty-three knots, getting on for twice as fast as Jessie's transport. It had nine decks to the Ionian's three.

Where it did not dwarf the Ionian was in the number of its passengers. It had about thirteen hundred as against the Ionian's complement of more than a thousand, with the main difference seeming to be the large numbers – some three hundred – in the Titanic's First Class cabins.

I move along from the display cabinet to another in which sits a log book. On the night of April14, 1912 it notes, three men were on duty at the wireless station at Cape Race about four hundred nautical miles from where the liner was positioned. That cape, I knew, was off the coast of Newfoundland and the Ionian bringing Cousin Jessie to Canada, could have rounded it too.

A minute by minute entry, written in a careful script similar to that deployed by Jessie and Hattie in the birthday book sets out in mundane detail the narrative we know all too well.

At 10.35pm it records a distress call received:

'have struck iceberg'.

Five minutes later:

'Titanic calls Carpathia and says we require immediate assistance.'

I cannot help but read on, even though everyone knows how this story ends.

At 12.50 a.m. a call is recorded from another ship, the Virginian:

'last he heard of Titanic was at 12.27 when latters(sic) signals were blurred and ended abruptly.'

I pause a moment before moving on. The room is silent.

In the next cabinet, I see a chair, a steamer chair, it's called – we'd call it a lounger. Here the passengers in First Class could put their feet up on their imagined pleasure trip.

The next exhibit shows the ghastly reality: it is entitled 'Shoes of the Unknown Child' retrieved off a two-year-old's body after being brought back to Halifax. It reminds me of that small figure peeping out from the back of the Yanaluk immigrant mother I had seen yesterday. Here is tragedy captured in two little shoes.

Two hundred and nine corpses were recovered from the North Atlantic and brought back to Halifax for burial. I read. These shoes are the remnants of just one small mite amongst the one thousand five hundred people who died in all.

The news of this disaster spread quickly around the world. It would have reached Cambridge just a week after Hattie Rooke died. Did it not make Jessie think twice about making the journey herself or did she really think she did not have much to lose? Perhaps she comforted herself with the old mantra that lightning doesn't strike twice in the same place.

Cousin Jessie accompanies me now as I move back to the main hall. We walk to the floor-to-ceiling windows to look out towards the calm twenty-first century waters shimmering in the Autumn sunshine. It may be warm outside but I seem to feel a chill – that chill of the North Atlantic in November, which might have hung heavily over Jessie's journey. Heavy it was with memories of the loss of all those souls, passengers, crew and small children, who died in those darkest of waters in that damned Spring.

Cape Breton Is, N.S, 2016

We have driven almost as far North as it is possible to go in Nova Scotia. We are spending the last couple of days of our trip here taking the Cabot trail which follows the coast of the Gulf of St. Lawrence, stopping every few miles to admire the breath-taking views. From some of the viewpoints, looking seaward you may, if you are lucky, spot schools of dolphins or whales playing in the still warm waters, or looking inwards, towards the mountainous interior of the Cape Breton Highlands national park, you may catch a lone moose on a ridge or see an eagle soaring above.

The road eventually leaves the gulf and cuts across the top of the island until we reach the sea again on the north-eastern tip near Cape North. There has been a lighthouse here for more than a hundred years, providing a beacon of safety to the ships, like the Ionian after their navigation around Newfoundland.

We drive on a few more miles and park up close to White Point. We set off by foot on the path across the headland. My braver companion, my daughter, is soon scrabbling down to the beach, while I stay above, gazing out to sea.

My thoughts have gone to Cousin Jessie again, as I realise this is the nearest I will come on this trip to her. I hope it was not too stormy when the Ionian sailed past Cape Race, heading for the safe channel between Newfoundland and Nova Scotia towards the calmer waters and safe haven of the Gulf of St. Lawrence.

I take long deep draughts of the ocean air, as I absorb the view as well as the ozone. The blue horizon holds no terrors on this warm holiday afternoon.

Tomorrow night we are going home. When Cousin Jessie passed close to this spot a century before, she would surely have been relieved to have survived the Atlantic storms but she was never going home.

After the lighthouse at Cape North, the next landmark Cousin Jessie might have seen was a solemn one. I have learnt from one of the handouts I was given at the Halifax museum, that the Ionian before it reached Quebec, would have made its first landfall at the quarantine station. This was on an island on the St Lawrence river called Grosse Ile.

A Celtic cross, more than one hundred feet tall, would have been an arresting sight for Jessie and her fellow passengers as they drew close to land. It had been erected just three years previously as a memorial to the thousands whose immigration journey got no further than this small island –

men, women and children, who died from disease not from drowning. The fear of contagion brought across the Atlantic was still very real for Cousin Jessie in 1912. This quarantine station was not closed until the 1930s.

My distant gaze and thoughts are brought back to the here and now by the sound of my daughter's voice. She is waving at me from the beach. I take some photos but decide not to join her there. Soon we will set off back to the car, in anticipation of our last night on Canadian soil – at least the last on this trip.

Cambridge, 2016.

I am back from Nova Scotia, even more determined that soon I must go to the West Coast. Amongst the few souvenirs I have brought back with me are some prints I found on a stall in Halifax for my uncle Ted. They are of an Atlantic convoy assembling in the harbour, taken sometime around 1941.

I want to go and deliver them in person as I hope to talk to him again, not just about his wartime service, but what he knew of my dad's. I know they talked in the way that men who had both experienced terrible things talked to each other, experiences they did not share, let alone boast about to others, not even to their own families.

There's another confidence they shared too. About an event they both attended forty years ago, thirty years after the end of that war; a ceremony in which they both had key roles –

and a pledge of secrecy I am convinced my uncle was vowed to keep, at least from me.

Sadly, I'm disappointed. He's not well enough to be visited at the moment, so I have to put the prints in the post.

I look at all the other photographs I took on the trip, the notes I have made, the new documents I have found and judge it a very satisfying trip. It brought home to me quite how arduous the immigration journey was for Cousin Jessie.

Every stage of it was potentially perilous and certainly exhausting: the long Atlantic crossing on a crowded and cramped steamship, with the treacherous ocean ever threatening; the stop at the quarantine station, tantalisingly close to Quebec and yet still so far. Then safe harbour finally reached, came the noise and chaos of the port, the hustle and bustle of the immigration hall, Jessie jostling with a thousand fellow passengers.

I see her trying to hold her own among the crowd, having her papers checked, getting provisions for the railway journey, checking her suitcase is on the station platform, getting on board before the whistle goes, with little time or opportunity to refresh herself, nor change her clothes. Then she's off again for seven days and nights on the train.

Finally comes journey's end, in a place which may have had the familiar name of New Westminster, but which was nothing like the London she knew. I hope the Munceys, William and Sarah, were there to meet her off the train.

Perhaps Jessie stayed with them at first, maybe even spending her first Christmas in her new country with them. It is only a hope though – I have no evidence yet that they provided any more than a poste restante address for Jessie, something to put on a form.

The immigration journey, hard as it was, was of course only the beginning. Nothing I have seen or read so far, gives me any confidence that a thirty-something woman. who had lived a modest life of service shaped by Victorian England could have been properly prepared for what might lie ahead now.

There's nothing to suggest she could face the future as a properly twentieth-century woman with the sort of assertiveness, swagger, and in many cases wealth that the Suffragettes had. No, Cousin Jessie was not that sort, I am sure.

I need to find out more about the organisation under whose aegis she travelled. In the margin of that immigration record I have now seen magnified and at close quarters are the initials G.F.S.

The more I find out about the Girls' Friendly Society, the more concerned I am for her.

Chapter Five

Kingsway, London, 2017

T rust in God – she will provide.

I am standing face to face with a large blow-up photograph of Emmeline Pankhurst and wondering whether Cousin Jessie would have been attracted to – or appalled by – her and her challenging suffragette slogans.

The portrait of this towering figure taken on a march, passionate and resolute, is redolent of the heady and turbulent time that coincided with Jessie's last days in England. It confronts me, as I step out alone from the glass-sided lift that has whisked me to the fourth floor of one of the LSE's university buildings in Holborn.

I have come to the home of the Women's Library, which is based here and which contains thousands of documents dedicated to women's struggles over the past two centuries. Housed here too is the archive of the Girls' Friendly Society, the organisation I now know was instrumental in getting Jessie to Canada.

From internet searches, I have learnt that the GFS enjoyed its heyday in the Victorian and Edwardian years, when it was run by formidable female stalwarts of the Anglican Church. With its network of branches throughout the United Kingdom and the British colonies, including Canada, its mission was to encourage girls and unmarried young women, especially those in domestic service, to improve their lot and do good works. Members – working-class girls – would be supported by Associates, who were middle-class women that often introduced their own servants into the organisation.

As the GFS's first historian put it in 1913: the organisation attempted to supply 'for every working girl of unblemished character a friend in a class above her own'. While always a female-managed and led organisation, it kept itself aloof from the women's suffrage movement. Its god, unlike Emmeline Pankhurst's, was no doubt male – and almost certainly British.

By 1910, the GFS had expanded its work to start encouraging young women – of unblemished character, of course – to secure a better life thousands of miles away from home. This was through an emigration programme to Australia, New Zealand and South Africa, as well as Canada.

From a twenty-first century perspective, it seems clear that the work of the GFS also served as part of the imperial endeavour to populate the British Empire with Anglo-Saxon Christian stock. My aim here today is to understand more about the organisation that encouraged thousands of young women, Jessie amongst them, to leave British shores for the first time, never to return.

I soon learn the etiquette of this archive. I have to put my bag in a locker. No pens are allowed, only pencils. I am relieved I am allowed to take in my trusty tablet, as well as an old-fashioned notebook.

As the librarian, having checked my identity, hands me a leather-bound volume of GFS annual reports, she is at pains to explain the care I need to take in handling this precious book. She gives me a pair of white gloves to wear and a soft bookmark to hold the pages flat, to avoid stretching the binding.

At my allotted desk, I am soon engrossed. The librarian comes over to my desk from time to time, looking over my shoulder rather nervously to check I am treating the book with proper respect.

I read with growing astonishment the annual immigration reports, with their often overtly imperialist tone. They were written by Head of Department, the Honourable Mrs Ellen Joyce. Over the five years leading up to 1914 she reports a growing and confident organisation sending an increasing number of young women abroad, their passage safeguarded by the GFS.

She displayed the numbers in neat charts that divided the emigrants into Servants and Educated women, including those travelling directly to be married.

In 1909 she wrote:

'It is most interesting to have interviews with young
women full of wit and intelligence balancing the love of
the old country weighted as it is with its plethora of
women, against the wider range of prospects of the
Colonial world.'

Weighted? A plethora? Presumably Mrs Joyce knew that a 'plethora' of something means a larger amount than you need or can deal with. This was of course even before the First World War decimated the population of marriageable men.

She continued:

'Applicants frequently write to ask which is the best place for the emigrant to go to. The answer should be Canada for choice, with assurance that in British Columbia there need be no fear of exploitation, that the range of employment in Canada is much wider and if there is not exactly the occupation the traveller is used to, plenty of other ways of leading a profitable and useful life.'

Mrs Joyce cautioned her colleagues against encouraging young women to go to the United States.

'It is greatly to be regretted that Associates do not give teaching in Imperial subjects… in these days, it is neither for the good of the individual nor the good of the Empire, that young women should go to the United States instead of Canada.'

She reminded her colleagues that the emigration scheme did not just benefit the young women, by offering them protected and subsidised passage.

'Every ticket taken through the Society increases our position with the Shippers, and, not only that, the commission paid to the Society, small as it is, forms the fund for working expenses.'

Mrs Joyce, whom I guessed would not have been a huge fan of Mrs Pankhurst, also seemed to be in a constant state of alert about the moral peril that might face her unblemished young women.

I have got the 1911 report before me now. As well as describing another expansion in the programme, Mrs Joyce reports she presided at a conference held at the Imperial institute with 'representatives from many societies interested in the safe Emigration of Women'.

This meeting had been called, it seems, in response to some alarming tales of inadequate protection for women during their voyages and on arrival (it is not hard to imagine what sort of misfortune might have befallen them). This was a particular problem, the conference heard, in the United States, providing further evidence for Mrs Joyce that the GFS's protected passage to Canadian ports was much to be preferred.

In her report the following year – the year that Cousin Jessie travelled – Mrs Joyce warmed to her theme. She stated that the number of GFS emigrants continued to grow, now topping a thousand a year, but she had a lurid warning for the young women who chose to emigrate without their protection.

'We may indeed be thankful for the Act repressing the horrible White Slave Traffic, but we must caution our girls more than ever not to listen to advice from strange women, for it is known that now wicked men have fled from England in fear of the lash… if caught at the wicked trade of luring young girls to destruction, wicked women are now taking their places.'

The White Slave Traffic! Really?

I thought that was a myth. I had to suppress a guffaw in the serious silence of the library. I did not want to attract the notice of that anxious librarian.

Mrs Joyce's report concluded that the young women of the GFS should be 'justly proud to be reminded that they are daughters of the Empire'.

Proud to be an imperial export – what, my cousin Jessie?

Perhaps. I need to think about that.

I close the volume quietly and return it to the shelf, where more leather-bound volumes await my inspection. These are the ledgers that contain the individual records of emigration.

It is a laborious task, not least carrying the weighty tomes to and fro from the shelf to my desk. I have to wade through several before I find the one I am looking for.

Here, at No. 2223, is Jessie Heading – and yes, it is the very same ledger entry I had been sent a copy of from the Canadian archive. Once again, I have to suppress my reaction, a whoop this time rather than a guffaw.

This very substantial document – its handwritten entries not photocopied, not digitally reproduced, but the real thing – delights me. The product of an Edwardian clerk's hand is vividly before me, fresh from transcribing the details Jessie had supplied.

So I read it again to absorb its impact – and import – once more.

Firstly, Jessie's big little lie: the stated date of birth is wrong by three whole years.

It is noted whether applicants were committed to the Church. Jessie's record contained several uncertainties.

Baptised – *unknown* (not now to me – Ha!).

Confirmed – *unknown*.

That's odd; surely Jessie would have known that, even if she didn't know whether she had been baptised as a baby. Maybe Jessie knew she was expected to be a committed member of the Church of England and fudged her answer.

Current address: *Bene't Street, Cambridge.*

She had left the job and the doctor's home where she had been recorded in the census the year before and was living in what the old street directories suggest was a lodging house close to the market and to her old home in Silver Street.

Her booking: travelling in Second class. The GFS's servants were clearly privileged not to have to slum it in Third.

Her sponsor, *Miss Borrer*, from the Cambridge branch of the GFS, introduced her to a *Mrs Sillitoe of Robson Street, Vancouver.*

Remarks: '*childrens nurse*' (*sic*). Noted for the immigration man and her Canadian sponsor, no doubt.

I carry on through the ledger and although I cannot find any more candidates from Cambridge, Mrs Sillitoe's name recurs repeatedly. It does not seem that she would have been Jessie's future employer. Rather, this stalwart of the Canadian GFS seems to have been merely a first port of call for young female immigrants.

Time for a break.

I feel I've achieved a lot in a morning but I am not done yet.

I get my bag out of the locker and take the lift downstairs, returning into a melee of students, who seem even more noisy than usual after my morning in silence. It brings me back with a bump into the twenty-first century.

I marvel again at how much the world has changed, not least for these young women around me now. How Jessie might have admired their confidence! Their comfortable, practical clothing!

Daughters of the Empire – certainly not!

After a hastily eaten lunch, I retake the lift to the fourth floor, greet Mrs Pankhurst again, put my bag away once more and prepare to plunge back into the distant terrain of pre-First World War England. As well as the GFS's national records, I have also ordered up some local ones.

By very happy accident, I have discovered the Cambridge records from 1908 to 1914 are also kept in this London archive. I pick one of these slimmer volumes carefully out from the box with my gloved hands and turn up the members' registration lists for the Cambridge North branch in 1912.

First, I see the name of Miss Evelyn Borrer, a committee member and GFS associate, as well as the sponsor whose name was on Jessie's immigration record.

Then my finger runs through the names of the ordinary members and yes, here she is – Jessie Heading, unmarried and presumed unblemished but hardly a girl. Maybe pretending to be three years younger than she actually was helped make her case for emigration?

I take another volume out of the box, this one for 1911. Here is Jessie again. Then I look back at 1910. Yes, she is there too, but not in 1909.

I flick through these Cambridge reports to see what Jessie might have done as part of the GFS group. I read that they meet regularly to do such good works as sewing and knitting toys for children in a London orphanage. Jessie's sewing skills were no doubt put to good use.

Then there were improving talks, including ones promoting the benefits of emigration, in particular to Canada. Clearly, Mrs Joyce's message got through.

I also read that GFS rules required that candidates for emigration had to serve time – at least two years, in fact – as members of the society before they could be recommended for protected passage. They did not want their young women to make rash judgments, evidently. Or perhaps they needed to observe their girls to ensure that their demeanour, conduct and godliness were up to the mark.

So Jessie had time to think what she was doing – and to be deemed suitable export material by her sponsor. It would seem Mrs Rooke's death in April 1912 was merely the final trigger for her to go.

Jessie Heading, illegitimate child, boarder, apprentice, housekeeper's helper, children's nurse, a sort-of-adopted daughter, and now accepted into the bosom of Mrs Joyce's embrace as a 'daughter of the Empire'-was she a woman fired by missionary zeal like Mrs Joyce or Miss Borrer?

Somehow, I doubted it.

More likely, I felt, my now not-so-distant cousin was someone at a low ebb, recently bereaved, without the security of family, on the shelf and with her biological clock ticking. Maybe she was beguiled by a dream painted by convincing persuaders, educated women, deemed her betters, whose comfortable lives in England they were unlikely to put at risk –'Trust in God, he will provide' amongst their comfortable mantras.

In these cathedral-quiet surroundings, with sunshine now streaming through the windows, I close the last volume and replace it on the shelf. I feel I understand the GFS a whole lot more now but do I understand Jessie any better?

The cousin I hope had travelled with a free and independent spirit, taking advantage of an opportunity for subsidised travel, could instead have been the victim of something closer than Mrs Joyce would ever acknowledge to being a sort of white slave trade – with one crucial difference, of course. Jessie had the freedom to escape.

I collect my bag for the last time, thank the librarian, pay my respects to Mrs Pankhurst and call the lift. It passes swiftly through the lower floors, packed with students at their desks, and then returns to the now quiet foyer.

I walk out into the street and am on Kingsway again, walking towards Aldwych. I can't help but remember that it is not the first time I have had a revelatory experience here.

Kingsway, 1996

I am walking into St Catherine's House, home of the General Register Office for England and Wales, where all the records of births, marriages and deaths are kept. I have managed to take a full hour for lunch and have slipped away from Channel 4's offices in Victoria, where I work.

I don't tell anyone where I am off to, let alone why I am going there. I am on a private investigation, a secret mission, you could almost say. I haven't yet told anyone apart from my husband what I have discovered in the past few months.

Mum had another breakdown a while ago and she has had to go into a home. I had to clear her chaotic flat in a hurry and take a mass of papers to my house for safekeeping.

We – Howard, our two children and me – moved out of London a few years ago, in part to be closer to Mum in Leicester. We now live in a small village in Cambridgeshire less than an hour's drive away. With work, commuting and family life, it takes me some time to get around to sorting out the drawer where I have stuffed Mum's papers.

Amongst the random collection of bills, rent books, pension and bank statements, recipes cut out from magazines, old birthday cards, letters and postcards sent by us to Mum from our summer holidays in Portugal and France (I tear my hair out at her inability to throw anything away or file things in some sort of order), I found a large brown envelope.

I opened it and inside were a whole lot of important documents dating back years: birth, marriage and death certificates, a will and some other legal papers. Some were routine and familiar, some made my jaw drop.

They have turned my whole understanding of my family relationships upside down. They explain my childhood – at last.

They are so devastating but, in some ways, unsurprising, that I can't talk to anyone about them. Certainly not to Mum. She's not well enough.

They have to remain a secret a while longer. For one thing, there are still things to find out – lines of inquiry prompted by the evidence in the envelope.

That's why I have embarked on this further quest, the one that I am now pursuing in my office lunch hour. I have ordered a record of a certificate of marriage up from the archive.

It is contained in a heavy leather-bound volume, and I now stand with it open in front of me at a page recording the details of a wedding in Leicestershire some time before I was born.

The handwritten records set down here devastate me to the core. They confirm what I had suspected after opening that envelope and reading the contents, undermining the ground that I thought my childhood was built on.

Now I realise it opens up new lines of enquiry – lines that I may struggle to follow. I certainly need some time to think about the implications of this wedding record, so I decide to leave it here for now.

I walk back to the office along the Embankment as I need some fresh air. I am rather good at keeping calm and carrying on but I need just a little more time to compose myself.

I return to the office and get on with my work. I have given my customary sandwich a miss, though.

Leicester, 1964

My dad is in a better mood than I have seen him in for some time. He has ordered a new car and it is being delivered today.

It's a Ford Cortina and will be the first new car he's ever owned. To house it, he's rented a lock-up garage around the corner. He doesn't want to risk exposing it to the elements, as his old Ford Popular had been, in the car park of the working men's club next door.

I've seen him filling out the hire purchase forms to buy it on our sitting room table. He does a lot of budgeting on that table, his brow furrowing as he calculates how, and in which order, he can settle the bills. At least he never has to worry about the rent, as our home is tied to his job.

When I see the car outside, I fall in love with it too. Unlike the old black Ford, this new car, which sits gleaming by the grey pavement, is a beautiful shade of pale mossy green. It's like seeing the transformation from black and white to Kodachrome.

Inside it has smart beige faux leather upholstery. I climb inside and stroke the armrest lovingly. I can hardly wait till we can go to the seaside in this marvellous motor but in the meantime the Saturday morning run to the shops with Daddy is much more fun.

It's only a ten-minute drive, but still – we are in our new car, our gleaming green beauty. Daddy likes to go to the greengrocer's and enjoys chatting with the man who owns the shop. Mr Biddles – a well-known man in Leicester, apparently – is also a boxing manager. They talk with great animation – I notice that, as Daddy never says much at home.

I don't join in the conversation, even though I have seen fights on the television and know who the champion of the world is. He's Cassius Clay, and he calls himself 'The

Greatest'. He's brilliant – handsome and charismatic, like a Hollywood star. He even dances in the ring.

After collecting the fruit and veg, there's a call at the butcher's to pick up the Sunday joint. Daddy likes beef best, but it's the most expensive, so he gets pork or lamb more often, and, very occasionally a chicken.

On the way back home, he leaves me in the car while he calls at the laundry, where he picks up his washed, starched and ironed white shirts, together with a brown cotton overall that he wears over his clothes in the club. When Mummy was ill, he'd used the laundry for all our washing, but that would be an extravagance now.

I'm looking forward to the summer holidays not just because of the prospect of a proper run in the Cortina. I'm saving up my pocket money to buy the new Beatles LP, whose release will accompany their first film. Both are called *A Hard Day's Night* and the film is going to be showing at the Odeon very soon.

One of the songs from it was released as a single a while ago. 'Can't Buy Me Love' was a big hit back at Eastertime, at the top of the charts for nearly a month. I know all the words by heart.

Say you don't need no diamond rings
And I'll be satisfied
Tell me that you want the kind of things
That money just can't buy
I don't care too much for money
Money can't buy me love.

Daddy likes the song too. As his taste normally tends towards Big Band sounds, this surprised me.

His favourite was Glenn Miller. In his rare moments of leisure, he puts his precious 78 on the turntable, which is encased in the same mahogany frame housing the wireless and which takes up most of the space on the wall opposite the sideboard in the living room. He sits down in his armchair and conducts along to the silken rhythms.

When his favourite track 'Moonlight Serenade' starts up, he goes into a sort of reverie... Doo... do... do... do, do... do... do, do... do... dooooo... do.

Perhaps it takes him back to a camp somewhere between Normandy and Berlin, listening to the angelic strains of Major Miller and his band on their weekly Army Forces Network broadcast, after another day in hell.

I knew something of Daddy's war service from Mummy – he never talked about it at all, nor ever showed me his medals. She told me he'd served as an engineer attached to the Desert Rats, as they were called after their service in North Africa. He'd repaired and driven tanks and other army vehicles, and done his bit in the retaking of Europe after the D-Day invasion.

She also told me that he'd heard his commander, Field Marshal Montgomery, addressing the troops outside Berlin and could never understand why, having battled across France and Germany, they were halted at the gates of Hitler's capital to allow the Russians to go in first.

Daddy was suspicious of politicians after that and he certainly had no time for Communists. He thought the new Labour leader, Harold Wilson, was a Communist too.

It was Mummy who told me nearly all I knew – or thought I knew – about my dad and how they'd met. It wasn't till after the war.

She was working as a shorthand typist in a small engineering firm in Leicester, when Daddy walked into her office. He was red-haired, handsome, and with something of Churchill in the set of his jaw, she said.

Love at first sight, it sounded like. All very romantic, like 'Moonlight Serenade'.

His name was Clarence Chesterton, but Mummy said his nickname was G.K. after the writer. She liked to think Daddy was related to him.

I had to piece together what happened next from random snippets Mummy let slip of their life before I was born. I wasn't sure what happened in what order.

I'd worked out that when she met Daddy, Mummy was past thirty years old, and he a year older. She was still living in the family house in Belgrave, along with two other older unmarried sisters.

She'd recently lost both her parents. Her mother had died barely two months after her father during the first summer of peacetime – of a broken heart, Mummy said. She'd been very close to both of them, so no doubt when this dashing ex-soldier came into her life, he filled a big hole.

I don't know what happened then. I assume they got married – probably not in Leicester, though.

I knew they'd left the city for a few years, come back before I was born, left again, then returned once more – all in the space of less than a decade.

At some stage there had been some time in London, in

Swiss Cottage. I didn't get any stories from their time there, so maybe it hadn't worked out.

Things seemed to look up when they went to the country, to live in a small village close to the Oxfordshire/ Buckinghamshire border. Mummy spoke warmly about life in the cottage in the Chiltern hills. Daddy worked for a furniture company in High Wycombe. He was on the committee of the works social club – Mummy had a newspaper cutting of that – and he played in the village cricket team.

Maybe Mummy worked as a typist there too, but she didn't mention it. They made some friends and it seemed they were enjoying the happy and relatively carefree life of a young couple.

Then I came along… and they went back to Leicester. I think Mummy was homesick and wanted to have her baby in familiar surroundings, close to her sisters.

Still sitting in our dreary sitting room in a house she seemed to hate and where she – and I – spent most of our days and nights didn't make sense to me, when we could have had fields to run in and cricket teas to eat.

So here are my baby photos, taken in Leicester and at the seaside. Here's me in a huge pram and a bonnet to keep the sun out of my eyes. Here are studio portraits and holiday snaps. Here are Mummy and Daddy holding me up on a wall as if I am a prize specimen – certainly their pride and joy.

All looks well. Yet soon they are on the move again with their baby. Here I am, as a toddler, pushing a trolley with a toy pony on it in the drive of a house, which Mummy tells me was in Yorkshire in another village, this time between

Bradford and Leeds.

From what I could gather, Daddy was still working for the furniture firm but as a 'technical representative', a travelling salesman, you might call it. I think I have a memory from that time: riding on the tram in Leeds – or did I imagine it?

Was it simply a story Mummy told me again and again, another happy time, with trams to ride on, rather more exciting than the red buses of Leicester?

By the time I am four, though, we have returned here. There must have been a change of plan as Mummy said they'd put my name down for a school in Pudsey, so why come back?

I wasn't sure that Mummy's explanation was convincing. She told me that Dad hadn't found the cricket club as welcoming as the one in Buckinghamshire. He wasn't a Yorkshireman, she said. Yet he didn't play any cricket at all once we came back to Leicester.

So I wonder now whether that was really the reason at all. Maybe Mummy was unhappy. Homesickness again? Or could it have been the prospect of lonely weeks stretching out ahead of her, with Daddy on the road and me at school?

Whatever, this time they seemed set on trying to settle. I was due to start school soon and, Mummy tells me, we moved into a house on the edge of Knighton, a very respectable Leicester suburb.

Mummy talked really fondly of that place, particularly as it was the first and, as it turned out, the only place they tried to buy together. I can't remember anything about this home and there are no photos.

I do have one memory of that time, though – a real one for

sure, and a happy one – well, for me at least.

I am sitting behind Daddy on a little seat as he cycles me to my new school. It's a bit bumpy, but it's fun as we rattle along. I am in my new grey gabardine school mac, with its belt tightly buckled to keep me warm, but the warmth I feel comes from sharing this rare adventure with him.

For Daddy, though, I realise now it was no adventure. Not at all.

It was an ordeal. The Suez Crisis is still talked of as a cause of national humiliation – for him it was a personal one. And for Mum and Dad both, it was certainly a crisis.

I know now that we were on that bike because of petrol rationing. It was no temporary deprivation, but precipitated the loss of Dad's job and the home of Mum's dreams.

That's how we'd ended up in a small flat above a pub in a poor part of town. Mum made a point of telling me that 'your father' had taken a job there and had said the only alternative to this comedown was for him to go back into the army – back to Germany, or even the Middle East. As he was past forty by now, I can't think that was a realistic option.

Still, Mum clearly thought it was a genuine threat. She'd gone along with it and the move to the club which followed – but in how she told the story, it was certainly with a heavy heart. Maybe she thought that Dad would leave us otherwise.

I don't think so – she had a ring on her finger, after all, didn't she? Till death us do part, wasn't that it? And I know Daddy would never have left me.

Jessie Heading with Mrs Harriet Rooke, Cambridge (c1890)

Jessie as a young woman, *carte de visite*, Cambridge
(c1895)

A young woman, likely Kate Muncey, London (c1908)

Mary McDonald, Leicester (1941)

Clarence Chesterton (c1943)

Above: The author with Clarence and Mary, Bridlington (1953)
Right: The author with a monkey (1961)

The author, with her mum and dad, at the seaside (c1955)

The author, with her dad and mum, at the seaside (c1965)

Above: The author with the Ford Cortina (1965)
Below: The author, Hillside Tennis Club, Leicester (1967)

Chapter Six

Cambridge, 2017

This is going to be the year I make it to Vancouver.

It's well into 2017 now and I am determined that my New Year resolution for this year will be fulfilled. The trip to Nova Scotia confirmed to me that I need to go and that I am ready to go.

My own sense, my understanding of Jessie's experience from being there, not just reading about it, has renewed and re-energised my wider quest. I am determined to find out more – yes and to feel more – about her life in British Columbia. The more I think about Cousin Jessie and her experiences, the more apprehensive I am for her... and yet, I know that, against the odds, she survived – and to a ripe old age.

I book a ticket to travel in late August and plan to stay for the best part of three weeks. I will base myself for the first week in downtown Vancouver and then will follow in Cousin Jessie's footsteps to the places I know she lived. I've bought a guide to Greater Vancouver and can find them all now within it.

Here's New Westminster, in Jessie's day a larger city than its better-known northern neighbour and still geographically at the centre of the area which is divided by the Fraser River. Then spread over several pages of the street atlas comes

Langley City: the area, first known as Langley Prairie, then as the rural township of Langley and now a sprawling suburb on the south-eastern edge of a twenty-first century metropolis.

I make a reservation at a hotel in downtown Vancouver, close by the Public Library, whose digital archives I have been trawling. I have more difficulty finding somewhere to base myself in the suburbs. I decide against hiring a car as I think I will see more if I go on foot as much as possible and use the city's extensive public transport network to cover the rest.

I need to find somewhere within easy reach of the two places I know Jessie lived in Langley. The only hotels I can find look dreary and are designed for business travellers with cars. So I settle on a bed and breakfast place which looks to be well-situated as well as offering more company and the possibility of acquiring more local knowledge as well.

I tell the woman who owns the B-and-B, Lorna, that I am doing some family history research and she seems genuinely interested. Sure enough, you don't have to go back far in her family to find English roots.

I try to work out as detailed an itinerary for my trip as I can while keeping some flexibility to allow me to follow up leads as I go along. I will start I hope with a visit to the Office of the Public Guardian.

I find a contact address on their website and fire off an email requesting to see the file of the Estate of William Underwood. I am hoping there will be more detail in it – and even some new evidence – more than I obtained in my correspondence with Mrs Jenkins. Unlike most of the other documentation I have needed for my research, this file has not been digitised.

I have to wait some time for a response but eventually I am given a name to direct my request to. I send off another email, this time to the Regional Manager. It takes a while to get a reply. He says he will request the file from the archive where it has been consigned and that it might take some time. I get the impression he is not exactly encouraging me to visit and he does not offer me an appointment.

Meanwhile, I try to work out how much time to spend in New Westminster. It is quickly reached from downtown Vancouver so I hope I might see all I need within a day.

I have already had to cross the Muncey residence off the itinerary. The handwritten address written on the immigration form, which appeared to say 'c/o the Burnaby P.O, Crescent Avenue' was not traceable by the local librarian I contacted. She had old city maps to call on, so is confident that there is not, and never has been a Crescent Avenue in New Westminster. She also tells me that an address I'd found for a William Muncey in a New Westminster street directory no longer existed. It seems back in 1912 he lived close to his work at a canning factory on 15th Avenue but his house had been demolished many years ago.

Still I do have at least one address to check out. In one of the digitised street directories for 1913 I found a listing for a Jessie Heading with the word Dom after her name, short for domestic servant, living at No.423 6th Street. I know the OPG believed that she was still in New Westminster in 1915 when William was born but there are no further listings for her after that first one.

As Mrs Jenkins told me that Jessie was Mrs McDonald by the time she arrived in Langley, I look for a Jessie McDonald in New Westminster but draw a blank there too, even though there were certainly plenty of McDonald men in British Columbia at that time. I find at least thirty living in New Westminster in 1914 alone.

I can find no evidence that Jessie met or married any of them. There's no marriage record and as there were no full censuses at that time, nor electoral registers, the street directories are all I have. I am stuck.

What if Jessie had moved to Vancouver though? I have little more than a hunch that this was a possibility – she might have wanted to escape to a nearby city with a baby born out of wedlock I reckon. It was not yet as big and important a place as New Westminster but it was growing fast. There would have been jobs there too, certainly after the outbreak of the First World War had taken away some of the male workforce.

A Canadian researcher, who I had contacted to help me with research there, knew her way around the street directories. While she also drew a blank for Jessie after 1913 in New Westminster, she did find this intriguing entry in a Vancouver street directory for 1915: *Jessie McDonald, widow of Donald, 1840 7th Avenue East.*

She sends me the link and I see it for myself. Jessie's still listed there the following year. By 1917 she has gone. Was this her? Had Jessie had a whirlwind romance, married, had a child and been widowed all in the space of two years? What was the chance of that?

The Canadian genealogist suggested that if she had married, her groom might have been one of the thousands of men who'd enlisted and gone off to fight in Belgium. This looked initially plausible – and romantic. Yet in the box file of Jessie's mementoes, there is no keepsake of a Canadian sweetheart who might have had an untimely death.

I am fortunate in the timing of my research: the Canadian military records from the First World War have just been released. I trawl through them but, sadly, I can find no Mc or MacDonald from British Columbia who died on the battlefields early on in the war and who was of a plausible age to have married Jessie.

I incline to a less romantic explanation. I feel it is more likely that my cousin had assumed the name, one which might have been familiar to her from her childhood and a name which as I had already discovered was very common in Canada, to create a new, more anonymous identity for herself than the more distinctive name of Heading allowed.

How and why she did this, how she came to have an illegitimate baby and how she survived on her own with a small child, become central questions for me to try to answer when I get to Vancouver. 1840 7th Avenue East goes on the itinerary.

I go back to the birthday book, which I am not going to pack – indeed I am not going to risk taking any of the most precious and irreplaceable items I have in the file – and re-check one of only two entries I am sure Cousin Jessie made when she was in Canada.

It is the entry for March 5th; in pencil and clearly handwritten over an erased entry, with the sort of smudging on the paper that a cheap rubber leaves behind: '*Willie Underwood, Born 5.15*' and then scrawled in underneath *'March'*. This form of recording a birth was quite different from others in the book. Was the rubbing out of William's actual birth name? Was this McDonald, Heading, or something else? Whatever, it seemed a strange way for Jessie to record what was surely for her the most significant of all the births in that book.

The only other Canadian entry? The death of a cat called Spot in 1946 is recorded. Did Jessie not make any friends in Canada? – or was she too busy making ends meet to record such details… and yet she found the time to register the death of a pet.

Was Spot her best friend after more than thirty years in her new country? I hope not.

Leicester, 1965

I would love to have another cat. We had a pure white one called, not very imaginatively, Tom, when we first lived here. I was desolate when he got run over on the main road at the end of our street. I remember crying at my old school and my teacher comforting me.

We do have a dog, called Rex, a black Labrador mixed with something else but he's not really a pet. He's kept by Daddy more as a guard dog and he lives outside in a kennel at the back of the scrubby space which we call the garden. If Rex ever gets taken for a walk, it must be before I wake up or after I'm in bed.

I would have liked a furry creature to cuddle today, that's

for sure. I can't be cuddling teddies any more – I've just turned thirteen.

I'm upstairs in my bedroom clutching a hot water bottle to my stomach instead. I've spent most of the day on the sofa downstairs, with a grinding pain in my belly which I've never had before.

I know what it is, even before the first spots of blood appear. Mummy does too.

I know about periods but not from her. My schoolfriends who've already crossed this particular threshold told me what to expect.

Mummy's just left the bedroom after a short and pained conversation with me. She's brought me a package, with some sanitary pads.

Her parting words to me were 'You're a woman now.'

These are words which puzzle me: I certainly don't feel like a woman or expect to be treated like a grown-up any time soon. Rather, in my parents my puberty will, I expect, set off increased anxiety about keeping me well away from what might now be dangerous male company.

My day-to-day life, I know, will hardly change at all, now that I am a teenager. I will still be ferried to and from school by my dad.

More and more of my time at home is taken up with homework, relieved by occasional weekend shopping trips. I've stopped asking whether friends can visit me at home: that's just how it is.

I don't ask to go out either. In fact, I can only remember one expedition I've been on in the past year.

Mind you, it's quite an outing – one which will keep me

going for a long time yet.

It was last October, when my classmate Jane had a ticket for sale. It was for a concert at the De Montfort Hall, which was only a short walk from school, the same place our Speech Days are held. On the stage, rather than a visiting dignitary and a few women wearing hats will be what they might call a popular beat combo.

Yes, of course, the Beatles were coming to town. The price to see them – seventeen shillings and six pence.

This is beyond the pocket of most of us girls, but without thinking quite how I would get this cash by the following morning, I told Jane I would take it. Rather I begged for it. I knew I wanted this ticket more than anything else in the world right now.

I asked my Dad on the way home whether I could go and if so, if he could give me the money, perhaps as an early Christmas present. He would have to think about it, he said – discuss it with your Mum.

More than the money, I think what worried him were the screaming girls, the crowds, the mayhem. He'd seen it on the news.

Maybe he could go with me... he mused aloud.

No, no, I was saying to myself – the shame of going to a proper pop concert with your dad!

I said I was sure there was only a single ticket – that the concert was a sell-out.

Well, he would have to drop me off as close as possible to the entrance and come into the foyer afterwards to pick me up.

Negotiations continued at home through teatime. The

decision would need to be made before Dad went to the club at six.

The answer was yes!

Oh joy! The cash was in an envelope by the time I went to school the following morning.

Maybe the sitting room drawer had been raided for the money put by for the next electricity bill or for Christmas. By break-time, I had in my hand a pink ticket.

I read the details carefully as if it were the most fascinating object in the world. There was a red stripe across the date: this very Saturday, October 10th.

Wasn't that the day after John's birthday?

I knew all their birthdays as well as those of my own family. He would be twenty-four! Quite old really.

Below that it said: 'First Perf 6.15p.m.'

I think the early performance time had helped sway Dad's decision. I could still be at home by nine and safely in bed by ten.

I read on.

'Arthur Kimbrell, Arthur Howes and Brian Epstein present…'

I didn't know about the other two, but Brian Epstein, I knew who he was – their impeccably spoken and smartly besuited manager. He was famous too.

Below that in capitals and bold black type was the proof that this was for real.

THE BEATLES SHOW.
C17
BALCONY – 17/6

The days till Saturday night dragged by but – at last – here I am now in the third row upstairs, to the left of the stage.

They come on at a run. They are in the same suits with the velvet collars they've worn recently on the telly.

The hall erupts into cacophonous rapture. They wave.

All the girls who love Paul (including me) think that he is waving at them alone. Ditto with the George, John and Ringo fans, although I can't think of more than one girl in my class who favours Ringo. The rest split pretty equally between Paul, George and John.

They take their positions on the stage. Paul with his left-handed bass guitar. (I note that – I am left-handed too). He is closest to my eyeline – couldn't be better – well unless I'd been in the front row of the stalls, of course.

Sweet-smiling George is to Paul's right. He assumes a more serious look as he focusses on his guitar.

John alone and on the other side of the stage assumes the role of Master of Ceremonies.

Ringo makes himself comfortable on the drums to the rear.

They begin – du, du, du, duh, duh, du-du-duh…The screams get louder, almost drowning out John as he rasps the first line:

'Well shake it up baby….

Paul and George respond…

'Shake it up baby….'

We all knew what is coming next. We could have sung along if we weren't all screaming so loud.

'TWIST… AND… SHOUT.'

Yes, we…I hadn't intended to, I hadn't dreamed I would, but swept up in that tidal wave of hysteria, I was screaming too.

Then comes the bit in the chorus where Paul and George shake their mop-top heads, go 'ooh' – and all we girls shake our heads in unison.

So it continues. Through their repertoire, which I knew by heart from my collection of Beatles LPs and singles:

'Money (that's what I want),' 'Can't Buy me Love' (as approved by Dad),' I'm Happy Just to Dance with You'...

The George fans are particularly pleased with that one as it allows the baby of the group, with the strongest Scouse accent, to take the singing lead.

Then a slower song and back to John:

'If I fell in love with you, would you promise to be true?

Yes, yes, yes, thought all the girls.

Then 'I wanna be your Man' gives Ringo the chance to take the lead.

John makes a joke. We still scream, rather than laugh – then on it goes:

'It's been a... Hard day's Night'...

Paul takes the refrain:

'When I'm home, everything seems to be right'.

As his voice climbs higher, the screams swell again.

'When I'm home, feeling you holding me tight, tight.'

By this time, I am so high on Cloud 9 that I'm not aware that in the stalls below me, the St John's Ambulance brigade are carrying a couple of girls, who've passed out, outside.

The boys start up again equally oblivious of the commotion.

A rip-roaring Rock and Roll favourite Long Tall Sally is declared to be the final number.

No, surely not, not so soon, we all think, the boys can't

leave us, not yet.

The screaming continues.

The boys, the fab Fab Four, take a bow. They wave and then they are gone.

The drum kit with The Beatles' name imprinted on the skin stands silent. The screaming and the stamping and the cheering dies away. Some girls are now crying, sobbing their hearts out instead.

I don't remember going down the stairs, what I said to Jane, or she to me, nor meeting up with my dad. I was in a daze.

The fresh autumnal evening air must have brought me round so the first thing I recall is Dad and I walking together briskly down the path from the entrance of the hall along by the park benches, each one with a partially-recovered overcome girl lying on it.

I recognise one of them – Jackie is in the class above me in school. Dad takes a dim view. He knew I wasn't that sort of girl.

What sort of girl was I? Who was I indeed?

Soon these questions will come to trouble me more. In the meantime, my life still swung to the regular rhythm of school terms and the release of the next Beatles record.

As to Mum and Dad, maybe I am getting more observant now that I am a teenager, but there seem to be more arguments. There was one terrible one, that I could hear clearly from my bedroom, late one evening when Dad came home after work.

It ended with the front door slamming and the morning after Dad wasn't at home. It must have been a Saturday night as I didn't have to worry about getting to school on my own the following day.

Dad was back in time to take me on Monday. I have no idea what the argument was about. I could tell my Mum was really upset. When Dad returned there was a chilly stand-off between the two of them. I was a go-between for a while – you know sending the 'tell your mother, I don't want any tea' sort of messages.

I knew it was serious. I sensed that my mother was afraid that Dad would leave us. So, although I did not see nor hear the reconciliation, I expect it was Mum who ended the stand-off first.

Mum never said a word against Dad to me, but I feel myself taking her side now. I am beginning to see the Working Men's Club next door, not as a magic place with a stage where I can perform, but as a dingy, smelly, beery place.

I spot what I think they call a 'girlie' calendar in Dad's office one day: a picture of a young blonde woman revealing her ample bosom, looking like a naughtier version of the starlet Diana Dors.

I am shocked and tell Mum. There's another row the next day and I feel I caused it.

I should be ashamed for sneaking on Dad, I suppose. Instead I start to feel Dad is not quite who I thought he was and that his world is not going to be mine.

Still all looks, on the surface at least, peace and harmony again by the time we go on holiday. Here I am standing by the Cortina in shirt and shorts. Here are Mum and I smiling on another beach by another pier.

Here we all are again at a family wedding, one of my

cousin's. Dad is in his best suit, waistcoat and bow tie, beaming at the camera alongside my mum in a cream crimplene suit and a red feather hat.

It is a black and white photograph but I remember the colour vividly as I do that of my bridesmaid's dress, burnt orange. It was a proper grown-up dress, full-length and with an elegant neckline, painstakingly handmade by the bride's mother.

Thirteen and a half, I'm growing fast (if hardly a woman). The boyish hairdo is gone. My hair is almost shoulder-length now, held back off my face with an Alice band.

I am also a different shape from the one I hated when I was eleven. That's not just happened by chance. I have started to take control of what I eat now.

I am trying harder at games at school and not being mocked by the P.E. teacher any more...and I am sometimes telling my mum I don't want much for tea.

I'm not thin enough yet though.

Leicester, 2017

A girlfriend of mine wants to visit King Richard III's tomb. His skeleton was famously discovered under a car park in Leicester five years ago and has been recently interred with much publicity in the cathedral.

This discovery of the skeleton of Shakespeare's villainous hunchback and last of the Plantagenet line, initially met with some scepticism, has been confirmed with the latest scientific analysis. After a scrap worthy of the War of the Roses between those who wished his Yorkist bones to return North and those in Leicester claiming finder's keeper's rights, it was my old home which won the battle.

I am pleased as I think this not-much visited Midlands city is in more need of a new tourist attraction. York would just have to make do with its Minster and its Viking and Railway museums.

I am happy to go along with my friend, especially as it will give me the chance to re-visit some of the places from my own childhood, which thanks to Cousin Jessie I have been thinking about lately. So we stand at the gates of the old Wyggeston Girls' School, now renamed and become a sixth form college.

We walk up New Walk to Victoria Park, and yes, there still in its pillared splendour is the De Montfort Hall. Then we walk the half-mile in the other direction down the tree-lined route towards the centre of the city.

It's a familiar path for me as Mum lived close by here after Dad died. I smile though to see the smart new tourist signs, pointing the way not to the cathedral but to its newest incumbent, King Richard III.

I divert a short way from the route the sign points us to, as I want to show my friend the offices in whose car park the skeleton had been discovered. I expected a plaque to have been put up but perhaps the Council which owns the site don't want crowds of tourists disturbing the officials who still work here.

When I was at school, this was seen as a pretty dull part of the city, lined with solicitors' and accountants' offices, with no shops to lure us this way. I did not realise then that it was in this very quarter where events had taken place quietly before I was born which would prove key ones in my life and that of my parents.

I knew now, of course, but did not share its personal significance with my friend, – not today. I haven't quite lost the habit of keeping my family secrets to myself. Secrets will out though – even those meant never to be told.

I am standing at King Richard's massive tomb which now dominates one of England's least grand cathedrals. Carved from ancient Yorkshire stone on a marble plinth, it is designed to last if not for eternity at least as long as the time that it has taken to rediscover his bones.

Richard's reputation, for so long disrespected by the Tudor-pleasing Shakespeare, has been largely rehabilitated too. His hunchback, once portrayed as the outer sign of inner evil, is now confirmed to have been a congenital deformity. How easy and damning those prejudices which we have only recently begun to shake off were!

In the afternoon, we leave the city centre and take a drive to the suburb where my mother was born a century before. It is reached via Leicester's version of the Curry Mile and now two-thirds of its residents are families of South Asian heritage.

We have no trouble finding the street where my Mum was born and went to school. It's in a surprisingly quiet spot, close to the old church of Belgrave where I was baptised.

We have a little more difficulty finding the McDonald family house less than a mile away where Mum spent most of her childhood and lived until the end of the war. I remember it as the place to which we walked occasionally to have tea with my two spinster aunts and an unmarried uncle who still lived there.

Thinking back, I am sure that he was what you would now call learning disabled. Mum's family never talked about that. All Mum said was that he was a surviving twin, his brother dying as a small child.

We drove slowly down the road of terraced houses.

'Yes, that's it', I say suddenly and my friend who is driving comes to a halt.

On the corner, here it is: number 56 – I remember it clearly now. Yes, there is the side door we used to go through, Mum and I.

Then we'd walk into the yard with the pretty knotted stone edgings to the narrow beds. There were always lily-of-the-valley blooming here in my memory.

It looks as if the house, which once contained Mum's large family is now split into flats. The side gate is locked and no-one answers the bell.

My friend takes a picture of me outside and we drive on. There is no time, at least on this visit to return to other places from my childhood.

Still, there's been enough time to honour my mum as well as a Plantagenet king, victims of prejudice both.

Leicester, 1966

Mum thought Richard III had been wronged.

She declares this one evening when we are watching Shakespeare's version of his life and bloody death on the BBC.

She tells me how my Grandma McDonald had told her how King Richard's corpse had been brought back to Leicester after the battle of Bosworth Field and, she said, dumped unceremoniously over a bridge into the River Soar.

Maybe it was because his body lay somewhere in the city Mum loved that she decided to claim Richard as one of her own.

Yes, she did love Leicester. I couldn't understand it – I suppose because I could only judge it from my own limited experience.

I knew Mum had left school at the same age I am now, gone to work and then enjoyed quite a social life. Since her breakdown two years ago, she has seemed relatively content in a world limited by the horizons of this Midlands city. Maybe she had come to terms with living within these four walls and on her memories.

Unlike me.

I know already that I won't stay here beyond school. I am going into the fifth form soon, starting my 'O' level course. The teachers are already beginning to think of our prospects.

Our formidable and never-married head teacher, Miss Pedley, expects her girls to get qualified so that we can sustain ourselves independently, whether we choose to marry and have children or not. We are encouraged to stay on at school after sixteen and then either get a good job with some proper training, like nursing or accountancy, go to the local polytechnic to learn something practical in art or design or, as in my case, aim even higher and go to university.

Those four young men from Liverpool have not just shown a new face of Britain to the world, they have shown the world to us fourteen-year-old girls as well. We see through them, Paris, Rome, San Francisco, New York, Tokyo and Sydney; the places they visit on their whirlwind concert tours look intriguing – and perhaps within our grasp too.

London, or Swinging London as it is now invariably called, is even more attainable. As well as all the pop stars who'd flocked there whether from Merseyside, Manchester, Birmingham or Glasgow – not just the boys, but Cilla, Dusty, Lulu and barefoot Sandi too, there were glamorous women in other fields.

There were the fashion icons, Mary Quant, Twiggy and the Biba lady, Barbara Hulanicki. Then there were brainy women on television and in politics as well, like Joan Bakewell and the red-headed Labour firebrand, Barbara Castle. I only had to work hard enough and I might enter their world.

In the meantime, my excitements come invariably from the telly – like this one.

I am on the sofa on a Saturday afternoon in late July. England are playing West Germany in the World Cup final. I don't normally pay much attention to football but for Mum and me this match is different.

It's two all at full time. Mum gets a cup of tea and says she's not sure she can bear to watch extra time.

So I am the only one in the sitting room shouting when Geoff Hurst scores again.

3–2!

Then in the final moments of the match, as some of the crowd start to celebrate, Hurst scores again... and the voice of the BBC says:

'They think it's all over – it is now.'

Mum comes back in and we cheer as madly as the Wembley crowd. We cheer again when we see our Leicester hero, the goalkeeper Gordon Banks go up to get his medal.

The following Monday, I find out he is coming back to Leicester to have what they call a 'civic reception'. I persuade Mum to come with me.

Walking from the bus stop, we are soon engulfed in another cheering crowd. He is on the balcony of the Town Hall which dominates the square.

We can just make out his figure and that he is waving, waving with those hands, the hands which the paper says are as safe as the Bank of England. Then, he turns around, goes back into the building and disappears from view.

It's all over. We go home and have our tea.

When I think about that day now, I realise, it was my mum's fiftieth birthday just two weeks before this celebration. I don't think we went out. I can't remember any visitors.

Did I even bake a cake?

Chapter Seven

Vancouver, 2017

The West Coast of Canada at last!

My two years of investigations are reaching their culmination. Here over the next two or three weeks all my laptop researches will come to life and be tested nearly five thousand miles from where my journey started.

I find Vancouver hot and sunny at the tail end of one of the driest summers on record. Forest fires are raging in the countryside not that far away and threatening to come much closer to the city.

Having arrived the afternoon before, and, of course, jetlagged, I start slowly and very much the tourist. I stroll to the Waterfront at Canada Place, where three large cruise boats are moored in the harbour, a couple of them bound for Alaska. Boats built and run for leisure, for entertainment, for a semblance of paradise, and which have little in common with the steamboats like the Ionian which had transported their human cargo across the Atlantic a century before. I imagine Cousin Jessie standing by me, marvelling with me at these gleaming white epitomes of luxury.

She has already joined me here in the city now transformed from the one she knew, a modest-sized city now a modern metropolis. Around us, tourists are taking photographs by the Canada 150 sign which celebrates the founding of the

Canadian Confederation in 1867. The selfie-takers pose against the multi-coloured maple leaf logo to show their friends they have been here.

Most of the tourists won't go further than downtown, then perhaps move on to the picture-perfect mountains or to Vancouver Island. My exploration is going to take me to the much less visited suburbs after I move on from here.

I leave the crowds on the waterfront behind and wander back towards the financial district, up Burrard Street. I am not yet used to the heat and take respite in Christ Church Cathedral. A place only the size of many parish churches in England, it is dwarfed by the office skyscrapers nearby and without my guide book I could easily have missed it.

Inside, it is quiet as well as cool. I ask the guide at the information desk whether he might have any pictures or leaflets about the first Anglican bishop, the Reverend Acton Sillitoe.

Sure enough, a few minutes later, a reference book emerges from under the counter with a photograph of him, along with his wife, Violet Sillitoe, Jessie's sponsor. It is taken in 1879 in London the year the couple married, he aged thirty-eight, she just twenty-four and before they set out to found the diocese of New Westminster. He sits in his clerical robes and dog collar, Violet, standing by his side wears an elaborate full-length gown with lots of lace and ribbons. She looks very much the Victorian lady with a tiny waist and with an elaborate necklace adorning her throat.

I doubt this was a dress she had much opportunity to wear once they had arrived in Canada. The frivolity of the dress contrasts with the severity of her face: Violet wears spectacles and has her hair pulled back tightly and unflatteringly off her face. She has a serious expression which speaks more of the hard life – well relatively speaking – they are soon to lead.

Later that day, I walk the length of Robson Street almost to Stanley Park and find number 1860, the address I have from an old street directory as that of Mrs Sillitoe. There is now a smart apartment block on the site, with replica carriage lamps, which hint at what it might have looked like in the years leading up to the First World War. By this time Violet was widowed and would have received here the many young women she sponsored on their immigration journey from the old country to the new, courtesy of the GFS.

As I stand in front of the building to take a picture, I see Cousin Jessie coming out of the front entrance. Over a cup of tea brought by her maid, no doubt, Mrs Sillitoe may have encouraged the younger woman to join the New Westminster branch of the society.

Perhaps she told of her own hardships when she first arrived. No doubt she wished Jessie well with her new life. A brief interview, a kindly goodbye, and then Jessie might have walked the way I am walking now back down Robson Street towards the train stop where she could catch the interurban service back to New Westminster.

Back in my hotel at the other end of Robson Street, I put in a call to the Office of the Public Guardian. I need to press my case for an interview.

The manager confirmed only a few days ago that the file on the Estate of the late William Underwood has arrived from the archive at last. He's told me he needs time to review it. He still seems to be holding off on offering me an appointment.

The Labour Day Bank Holiday is coming up and I am

worried that he might try to put things off till after the long weekend. I cannot wait that long.

I explain that I am only in Vancouver for a week. I know the man from the OPG doesn't realise quite what a mission I am on and that I am not to be easily deterred. Finally, he agrees to an appointment at ten a.m. on Friday morning in two days' time.

Thursday passes in a flurry of tourist activity to distract me from the anticipation of what I know should be a key day of discovery. I still feel befogged by jetlag, so I am hoping my head will clear by tomorrow.

I buy a sunhat as if that might help. It is much warmer than I expected and I hope to relax a little before the big day.

On Friday, I am up early – jet lag at least has the advantage of making this easy. My mind is focussed but I feel nervous.

I dress myself smartly as if preparing for a business meeting. I decide to walk the few blocks from the hotel and set off with my iPad and old-fashioned ring-binder notebook in good time to find the unassuming building on West Hastings Street where the OPG conducts its business.

Inside the lobby, I find that it is one of those offices with super-secure lifts where you need to have the receptionist put in a smart card to allow you up. The lift silently and speedily takes me to the seventh floor where the OPG's manager is waiting for me, with a large file under his arm.

He ushers me to a small windowless conference room. I get the distinct impression, that this will be a business-like rather than a friendly meeting and suspect that I will only be allotted an hour of his time.

I expect he is not used to requests like mine nor meetings

like this. I am sure Mrs Jenkins would have been a little less guarded. I mention her name and say how helpful she was, hoping that will ease the atmosphere but he does not respond. Perhaps he did not know her.

I ask first whether the file he has now thumped down on the table is the whole record of the case of the late William Underwood. No, he says.

It seems he has thought hard about what I am entitled to see. It is, he explains, the file which had been submitted to the Supreme Court to make their case in settling the Estate of William Underwood. I realise that what I am to see is no special privilege – it is in fact a public record but I expect that I am the first to request it and the first to see it since the case was closed six years ago.

He now opens the file and says he will pass me the contents a page at a time, having checked each one first. Given my instinct that we might have just an hour, I decide that this could be a laborious and time-consuming procedure if I try to read the contents as we go along.

If my time is limited, I need to make sure we get through the whole file. So I put a question to him: can I take photographs on my iPad as we go along?

There is an anxious pause but at last he says yes. That's a relief, but I try not to look too pleased.

He also says he will give me a short commentary as we go along. I nod in acknowledgement and thanks but I decide not to ask more than the odd question as we proceed – not just to keep things moving but because I don't want to reveal to him how much I know already. I sense that he doesn't entirely trust me.

We begin.

In swift succession, an array of photocopied documents passes from his to my side of the table. As I take photographs, I try to register which of them I have seen before. Even if they are familiar to me, I decide I will still photograph them. Again, I don't want to faze him, as this might reveal my prior knowledge.

So, first out of the file is William's death certificate. New to me, even though I knew the details. No birth record though, I silently note.

I am quietly astonished by the second Court exhibit. They are a couple of scanned pages from the birthday book. Yes, that very same book which is still sitting in a box in my Cambridge study.

I don't mention this to him – and there is no sign that he is aware that his predecessor sent me the book along with all the other treasures. The two pages kept in the file record Jessie's January birthday and William's in March. This latter, when photocopied, looks even odder than the original. The clumsy erasure stands out even more but, frustratingly, the original entry below is still illegible.

Next comes a probate document from 1970 setting out the assets that Jessie had bequeathed to her son and Jessie's will, dated 1942. A property in Langley comprises the bulk of her estate. Definitely worth poring over later.

Then comes paperwork relating to the grant of powers of attorney to the Office of the Public Guardian in the early 1990s and the Court Notice which brings their work to an end in 2011. New documents but unlikely to be of interest to me now.

Next comes Jessie's family tree but this time with nothing

redacted. Those missing spouses are revealed at last – although this information is mostly irrelevant to my investigation.

Three reports by different genealogical researchers from 1995 through to 2008 follow. Very interesting.

Then, a document from England, seemingly a product of one of those genealogical investigations. A will, dated 1913, just a few months after Jessie had arrived in Canada – Mary Ann Heading's.

For the first time this morning, I can hardly contain my feelings. As far as the Supreme Court was concerned, this exhibit provides essential evidence that Jessie was indeed Mary Ann's daughter.

For me, it demonstrates something else entirely. My finger starts to shake as I press the virtual button on the iPad to take an image. It shows without doubt that Cousin Jessie's natural mother may have given her up at birth but far from disowning her illegitimate child, she remembered her with a legacy.

My mind floats out of this airless office to two others back home and in another time.

Sandy, Bedfordshire, 1913

So this is how it was.

An elderly countrywoman visits the offices of a provincial solicitor on a February day. She has important business to conduct.

Having inherited money from her father, William

Heading, she has been living comfortably for the years since his death in this Bedfordshire town with other respectable ladies of a certain age. Close by, lives and works her favourite nephew, John McDonald. He is well-known in the local community as he runs the butcher's shop in the High Street.

Now in her sixties, she is persuaded that it is time to make a will. She will make John Executor and leave him the bulk of her estate but she will also remember some others.

These are her wishes, carefully handwritten.

'*This is the last Will and Testament of Mary Ann Heading of Sandy, in the County of Bedford, Spinster. I revoke all prior Wills made by me. I give and bequeath the pecuniary legacies following (namely) to my daughter Jessie Ashbowl Heading the sum of Forty pounds. To my sister Elizabeth McDonald, the wife of John Moore McDonald, the sum of Forty Pounds To my sister Fanny Mackness, the wife of Original Mackness the sum of Forty pounds*'...

It is signed in her own careful hand and witnessed by Edward Sills, her solicitor and by his clerk. Along the left-hand margin is John McDonald's signature.

This is how this spinster remembers the child she gave birth to thirty-six years before, bequeathing the same amount to her as to her eldest sister, my great-grandmother McDonald. There's another forty pounds for the sister whose son she looked after, once her now-remembered daughter had been given away. That son does not receive a legacy from her.

Mary Ann Heading will live for another twenty years.

Leicester, 1956

So this is how it was.

A forty-year-old man attends the offices of a provincial solicitor on a March day. He has important business to conduct.

Clarence Chesterton has been living for a couple of years in Yorkshire, with Mary and his young daughter. The family has recently returned to Leicester and today he has an appointment in Millstone Lane, where Arthur Headley, Solicitor and Commissioner for Oaths, has his office in the lawyer's quarter of the city.

Even though he is still a youngish man in good health, he is persuaded that he should put his affairs in order. He is not a rich man, far from it, but he is planning on buying a house. The solicitor has advised that Mary should be not only Executrix but also Trustee of his property with his three-year-old daughter, the sole beneficiary.

This is what his wishes are as set out in a typewritten document on thick cream-coloured paper.

In bold capitals it declares:

'I GIVE DEVISE AND BEQUEATH all my real and personal property whatsoever and wheresoever situate at the time of my decease UNTO my Trustee UPON TRUST as to my real property for sale and as to my personal property to convert the same...into money...and to pay thereout my debts funeral and testamentary expenses...and to stand possessed of the residue for my daughter Fiona Mary Chesterton as and when she shall attain the age of Twenty one years AND I DECLARE that it shall be lawful for my Trustee at any time... to raise any sum or sums out of the capital of my estate and apply them for the advancement and benefit of my said daughter... during her minority in such manner as she shall think fit. IT being my desire and intention that my said estate shall be utilised as far as possible to give my said daughter the best start in life which my estate is capable of providing for her.'

No provision is made in the will for the Executrix.

It is signed C H Chesterton and witnessed by Hector McDonald, my Uncle Hec of Belgrave Road, Leicester and by Mr Headley's Clerk. He has signed a typewritten slip which acknowledges receipt of this last Will and Testament, 'to be placed in my strong room for safe custody.'

The trust is never put into effect but the will is never revoked.

My dad will live for another twenty years.

Vancouver, 2017

No more time to waste. I reckon half an hour has passed already – no time to get too distracted by the implications of just one of the documents before me.

Next!

The file now produces some correspondence from 1995 and 1996, at the start of the OPG's long investigation into the case of William Underwood deceased. This is between another of the predecessors of the man sitting opposite me now and the Vital Statistics department of British Columbia, the equivalent of our Registry of Births, Marriages and Deaths.

It refers to several unsuccessful searches. These are new too, I realise.

Then there is something I really wasn't expecting at all: a typed transcript of a conversation between William and a carer in a Langley Nursing Home and a handwritten note from 1992 of another conversation between these two. Now these might indeed be interesting.

Then another surprise: a handwritten letter dating from the year after William died, in 1995, from a woman called Mrs Kerr, describing Jessie's arrival on the prairie with William. It is a witness account apparently – very interesting indeed.

The word 'illegitimate' stands out from the page. That word again.

Then more routine stuff: Jessie's birth and death certificates, but not the baptism record, I had unearthed in Cambridge, which had revealed to me the name of Jessie's father. Certainly better not to mention this – I know the case is closed but I don't want to rock the boat, with a new line of descent I had uncovered from Richard Ashbowl Crisp to William.

We get to the end of the file a few minutes before eleven and the man from the OPG is clearly keen to go to his next meeting. I feel he might give me the time to answer just one or two questions at most.

I settle on what appears to me still to be a gaping hole in the file: the lack of evidence around the circumstances of William's birth. There was no record that had passed my gaze in the past hour, I was sure.

What accounted for the lack of a birth certificate I ask?

The answer: there were a lot of wooden buildings and a lot of fires at that time in British Columbia. The document could well have been lost that way he implies.

I did not express the scepticism I felt at that answer. He also seemed confident that William had been born in the hospital in New Westminster – and why? Because that's where William told the carer he'd been born. His mother Jessie had told him it was in the hospital built by convicts.

So was that the Royal Columbian I ask? Yes, that's right, he confirms. I told him that as I knew the old hospital had been replaced by a very modern building, I wasn't planning to go there on my travels.

So that was it. Unless I had missed something the only evidence that William had been born on the date and in the place he said was from a pencilled and clearly altered entry in a birthday book and from the uncorroborated testimony of a frail elderly man in a nursing home.

I wasn't sure why the OPG was so confident that this was convincing. Still the Supreme Court had been happy, so who was I to dispute it… and of course, I had benefitted directly from that court's judgment.

It would be churlish of me to challenge it – but I am a seeker after truth: the truth of Cousin Jessie's life and who she was. This official doesn't understand this – why should he?

After an hour of this blizzard of paper, and hurried taking of photos, I emerge somewhat overwhelmed, my head aching from that and from the airless room. The manager bids me a polite farewell as he sees me into the lift.

As I return to the ground floor, I am elated but also somewhat frustrated. There's a lot to be read later, I realise, but it is a shock to have confirmed that I know rather more about Jessie than the OPG or their genealogical researchers ever looked for, let alone found.

I'm already kicking myself that I did not find the opportunity to interrogate the manager on why the investigation took seventeen years. That's still the question most friends ask when I tell them the story of the windfall inheritance. Maybe reading the reports in the coming days and more than that, following in Cousin Jessie's footsteps, will help me find the answer to that question as well as the ones I find more pressing.

I walk out of the building, clutching my iPad even more firmly. Emerging from that dark conference room, the August sunshine is blinding.

The city streets are quiet. It seems many workers have already left for the Labour Day weekend. I walk on the shady side of the street in an urgent search for coffee.

Back in the hotel, I know I want to get outside straightaway and enjoy this lovely late summer day. I go quickly through my digital record of the OPG's file. Yes, the photos are all there.

My eyes pause on one of the handwritten documents which has most intrigued me. This letter, which became Court Exhibit K, was written on March 17, 1995 and addressed to one of Mrs Jenkins' predecessors at the OPG.

A woman called Velma Kerr had written from Langley, B.C. in response to the OPG's request for information about the family of the late William Underwood.

'When a young child I lived with my family on a farm in Milner ajoining(sic) the farm of the late George Underwood. Mr. Underwood was a rather elderly batchelor (sic) who had lived on that farm for many years. One day a lady arrived on his farm with her young son who was about five years old. Her name was Mrs McDonald and her son's name was Willie. They came from Vancouver. Mrs McDonald remained to be Mr. Underwood's housekeeper. Willie went to school for several years in Milner. Mr. Underwood became old and shortly before he died Mrs McDonald had the minister for the local church come to the house to marry her and Mr Underwood.'

A paragraph followed about the elder man's family and addresses where they might be contacted. There were no kind words about Willie nor his mother.

My eyes move on to the next sentence which is on a line to itself.

'It was no secret that Willie was an illegitimate child.'

Then... 'Willie and his mother lived together in a small home in Langley City after leaving the farm after Mr Underwood died.

They made few friends...'

Enough. No, too much.

Chapter Eight

Victoria, Vancouver Island, B.C, 2017

L abour Day Monday and time for a break.
After the welter of revelations at the Office of the
Public Guardian, I need to clear my head. I have booked a
day trip by seaplane to Victoria.

Still jetlagged, I didn't find making an early start from
Vancouver too painful. Now at just half past eight I am
gazing out from the plane window to see the capital of British
Columbia taking shape gradually before me through the early
morning mist.

It is very seductive – and calming – to be lured away from
my investigations into full-on tourist mode. Having walked
miles around Vancouver over the past two holiday days,
taking in Stanley Park, Granville Island, City Hall, the Steam
Clock and the rest, ticking off the attractions in my
guidebook one by one, this will be the last day I allow myself
time off.

We land before most people will have had their breakfast.
The passengers disperse quickly and I walk towards the
landmark building on the other side of the harbour area,
which I work out from my guide book must be the
Parliament.

The mist has dispersed and with the sun now blazing, the
view across from the airport looks not unlike a sedate English

seaside resort in its prime at the start of a glorious summer's day. There's no pier but there are formal floral displays mimicking those grand seaside lawns in Scarborough and Eastbourne. An imperial-grade hotel, the Empress, sits in pole position with the best sea view.

I divert from the roadway, walk up the drive and take a peek inside. I decide against breakfast but consider whether I may return in time for the full English-style afternoon tea on offer later. Turning from the poster showing the teapot and the scones, my eyes alight on a display of black and white photographs on the wall outside the dining room. It's celebrating the hotel's founding in the Edwardian era, just a few years before Jessie's arrival in the province as one of the so-called 'daughters of the Empire'.

I walk out of the hotel, down the steps, back to the road, and carry on walking towards the even more grandiose Parliament. Presiding over the scene is the Empress herself, Queen Victoria, and before her the letters of her name are picked out in a carpet of red flowers.

Behind her, the Parliament, a neo-Baroque pile, stands in suitable tribute. I take the tour and duly admire the rotunda and the empty legislative chamber (the legislators being on holiday too).

Coming back outside onto the grassy square after an hour, a more relaxed mood appears to be overtaking the area. There is a stage with a band warming up. Families are crowding into the area, with picnic bags and excited young children. People are getting out camping chairs, looking as if they are preparing for a long afternoon. Gazebos shelter beer and food stalls, which are beginning to do a brisk trade.

The band starts up and some of those gathered around are already clapping, swaying to the rhythm, even properly dancing. From this angle, Victoria's back appears turned – probably a good thing.

I am beginning to feel my very early start from my Vancouver hotel, so I sit down on the grass and succumb to this more relaxed West Coast vibe. It may not be San Francisco, nor Laurel Canyon, but there's sunshine, the Pacific Ocean and live music, and it doesn't take much of a leap of imagination to take me back to 1967, the Summer of Love.

Leicester, 1967

I have it at last! I am clutching a new LP that I have just bought from the record shop. It is a thing of beauty and I turn it over and over carefully in my hands.

The cover is a work of art, for sure. In the centre are John, Paul, George and Ringo, dressed up in multi-coloured satin Ruritanian-style military uniforms, carrying not guitars but instruments that our school brass band might play.

In front of them, not Ringo's usual kit but a single drum that looks more like something out of a fairground, with gilded letters embossed on the skin spelling out their reincarnation as Sgt Pepper's Lonely Hearts Club Band. Around them is a sea of faces and figures, framed by a full-size model of a black boxer in a satin dressing gown to the left and on the right, in their evening gowns, a strange couple not seen previously together – the German Marlene Dietrich and the British star Diana Dors.

I recognise some of the other faces incongruously brought together: here's Marlon Brando, Fred Astaire, Bob Dylan. Is that Lewis Carroll? Lawrence of Arabia? Oscar Wilde?

Immediately to their left are the wax models from Madame Tussauds of the Fab Four, as they were just three years ago, when I was a child and screamed at them at the De Montfort Hall.

In front of this bizarre montage is a floral display, with the word 'Beatles' spelled out in red flowers, like one of those displays in seaside parks I have visited, or maybe it's supposed to be a graveyard. Not a Christian graveyard, though: there's some sort of Oriental china doll and a Hindu statue here too.

I turn the cover over. Here are John, George and Ringo in their mock uniforms and moustaches again, with Paul's back turned.

The rest of the space is taken up with all the lyrics from the cornucopia of tracks awaiting to be revealed on the disc within the inner sleeve. I start reading from the top left:

'Side One, *Sgt Pepper's Lonely Hearts Club Band* – It was twenty years ago today…'

and then look down to the bottom right-hand corner to see how it ends… 'A Day in the Life: Now they know how many holes it takes to fill the Albert Hall. I'd love to turn you on.'

The BBC's banned those words from the radio and TV. Apparently, they mean something to do with taking drugs, not 'turn on' as in putting the telly or the radiogram on. 'Found my way upstairs and had a smoke' has a double meaning too, it seems... and every word of 'Lucy in the Sky with Diamonds', apparently.

I don't care about any of that and I certainly don't know anything about it. I am just intoxicated by the music: the whole sweeping, glorious fairground ride of it.

I play it for the first time now in the sitting room on the big mahogany-encased record player. I am alone – where is Mum? In her bed again perhaps, or in the kitchen? I am lost in a world of my own anyway: I will play it over and over again this summer until I know every word and every exhilarating bar of it.

Dad's gone off the Beatles now. He thinks they've gone to the bad, with their long hair, their spikiness – particularly that cocky Lennon saying that the band is 'more popular than Jesus'; the trips to India to stay with strange, white-robed gurus; their partying, consorting with what he judges to be even worse types like the Rolling Stones.

Gone to the dogs. Where will it end?

I think he's afraid for me and my innocence. He's noticed too that I'm keener these days on Lennon than McCartney, who he still has some time for.

Yes, I've left Paul behind after a long first love, and now am besotted with his naughtier best friend.

I'm positively pleased that he's not the sort of boy that Dad and Mum approve of – although, of course, they wouldn't allow either of them through the front door. As for real boyfriends, they are as remote as ever, although I have at last discovered one way to meet some boys through my other summer passion. I have joined a tennis club.

Neither Mum nor Dad play, so there's no risk they will

want to come along too. I developed my enthusiasm for the game at school but I doubt I'll ever make the school team. I suspect I'm still seen as the formerly fat third former who was hopeless at games and can safely be pigeonholed as a clever, bookish girl who's invariably top of the form.

For my birthday this year, I asked Mum and Dad for a proper racquet and am now the proud owner of a state-of-the art Dunlop Maxply Fort. At first, I practise with it in the car park of the Working Men's Club, hitting a tennis ball for hours against the side of our house.

I persuade Mum and Dad that if I am to improve further, I need to play proper games. I discover that there's a club called Hillside just ten minutes' drive or a manageable walk away. There's a really cheap subscription too for junior players and they let me sign up. Somehow there's money for a tennis outfit too: a white poplin dress, fitted to my increasingly petite frame. I'm all set.

I soon start to make some new friends, the first people I've ever properly met outside my school or family. There's a girl called Julie, who's at a local secondary modern, and two boys, Stuart and Michael, who attend one of the city's grammar schools. They're all rather better players than me, but they're happy to accept me as their fourth player to make up a double.

At the end of one afternoon, Julie asks me my exact address. I tell her without thinking why she wants to know.

The next morning, with no warning, she turns up on the doorstep. My mum goes to the door, before I can get there. I expect Julie must have taken her breath away with the shock of seeing this stranger, this fifteen-year-old girl with a tennis racquet standing outside, asking for me in a broad Leicester accent.

Mum does not invite Julie in. I scramble to get myself ready quickly so as not to leave my new friend too long embarrassingly on the doorstep.

This will turn out to be the only time Julie – or indeed any friend, female, let alone male – pays a call here.

You see, Julie was banned from our house as a result of what we got up to shortly afterwards at the club.

After a match with the boys, they invited us to go for a walk with them.

In my memory, it was idyllic countryside we meandered through (or what I imagined to be such, as I had never been on a country walk before).

In fact, it was simply into the wilder edges of a local park that I was unfamiliar with. It was a hot August day and we four fifteen-year-olds held hands in two couples, and in the quietest spot of our walk, under dappled sunlight, kissed under the trees. Nothing more – we had to get back to the Club by six o'clock, when Dad was due to pick me up.

He knew something had gone on without having to ask too many questions. I still don't know how.

Maybe there was a new flush in my face. I expect I was a pretty poor liar when asked how I had spent the afternoon and whether I had won the game. I'd had nothing to hide from him before, so it wasn't that hard to get the truth out of me.

Well, part of the truth, anyway – the walk in the park, but not how it had ended. I think Mum blamed Julie – I expect she'd decided my friend was a common type.

Dad was angry, really angry – maybe as much at himself as me, for allowing me into this sort of temptation. Fortunately for my parents it was not long till our summer holiday, this August in a caravan on the Yorkshire coast. School would start again immediately upon our return.

That was the end of that. There was to be no return to the Hillside Tennis Club.

It wasn't the only row I remember that summer. Maybe it was another thwarted attempt on my part to escape the strictures of home. I cried and raged, and then a question came out of the depths of me, out of my semi-conscious self, that surprised me as much as it did my mother.

'I don't know who I am,' I said.

'What do you mean?' said Mum.

'Who am I?'

Silence.

It was like a new, updated version of my plaint as a ten-year-old, when I was convinced I had been adopted. Mum was speechless. She didn't understand what on earth was wrong with me.

Eventually she stuttered out something about being her daughter – and Dad's. That is not what I meant at all.

Gulf of Georgia, B.C, 2017

I am on the ferry boat back from Vancouver Island to Vancouver itself and as the national holiday draws to a close, my thoughts return to the working week ahead. In my case, it means returning to the search for Cousin Jessie.

I am contemplating how easy it might have been a century earlier for her to change identity – to try to become someone else. My meeting in the OPG has made me realise that that is what her emigration journey allowed her to do.

Jessie Ashbowl Heading could become Mrs McDonald if she so wished without any trouble at all. No identity documents required.

Date of birth? Well, flexible. I am who I say I am.

I have a reference from a bishop's widow. I can be a children's nurse. I can be a housekeeper. I can be a farmer's wife.

I can read and write. Here is my signature, Jessie A. McDonald.

I can speak quietly and politely in the English way.

I have good manners as I have lived in the households of gentlemen and gentlewomen all my life. No airs and graces, though. Just call me Jessie.

Is that how it was?

I decide to do some work now and skip dinner. There is a huge queue in the restaurant and the boat is heaving with passengers at the end of the long holiday weekend. I find a quiet spot and get out the iPad again to review more of the documents I've copied from the OPG file.

My eye alights on this. It is Exhibit C to the Supreme Court of British Columbia and comes from a man called Ian Hilder, described as a genealogist and probate researcher, with an address near Lewes in East Sussex.

It was written in February 1995, less than a year after the death of Jessie's son William Underwood. Here was the first of the heir hunters, it seems.

Mr Hilder is reporting back to the OPG about the results of his investigations so far. It follows on from a previous letter, also in the file, revealing that he has uncovered Jessie's true birth certificate in the English archives (yes, but not her baptism record. Ha! I think, recalling my triumphant discovery in the Cambridge library).

He refers in his report to the marriage certificate he has received from Canada – the record of Jessie's wedding, not to a MacDonald, but to the farmer George Underwood.

He writes:

'We were pleased to hear that you have evidence which suggests that the Birth Cert. that we provided for Jessie Ashpole (sic) Heading is the one you were seeking.'

I realise that Hilder, having no access to the baptism record, would not have seen Jessie's middle name written as Ashbowl. I know very well now just how fluid names could be a century ago; written down with two or more spellings.

The same confusion applied to MacDonald, or was it McDonald, as it appears in another document, a letter, in the OPG file. Who could know now which was correct?

Mr Hilder goes on to say that if he had the correct birth record, then the information that Jessie supplied regarding her parentage at the time of her marriage in 1920 was false and that any other family information given by her should therefore be treated with suspicion.

'Suspicion' – that's the sort of word that would be easy to use of someone who was illegitimate and a domestic servant, and who, it seems, had an illegitimate child within three years of arriving in her new country. If not from the criminal classes, she certainly wasn't a lady.

Marrying a seventy-six-year-old man might surely be suspicious too. Mr Hilder did not consider that Jessie might have had reason to invent a father called Heading, declare his wife to be Harriet Rooke, take a few years off her age and seize an opportunity for security by marrying a farmer – however old – in the prairie community she had somehow arrived in.

Tomorrow I will go to New Westminster, where Jessie's British Columbian adventure began – the city declared as her intended destination on her immigration form and the place in which the Office of the Public Guardian believed her son was born.

Enough for this evening, though. I must take in the view from the boat as the sun sets off the western horizon, amidst the seemingly floating islands that lie between here and Vancouver.

The sunset is mesmerizingly beautiful.

New Westminster, B.C, the next day

Back to business. Holiday over, and along with the commuters, I am taking the Skytrain from downtown Vancouver to the suburb of New Westminster.

The old streetcar service between Vancouver and the once

bigger and more important city, which Cousin Jessie would have known, has long been closed. This new line over the city, a legacy of the Expo exhibition thirty years earlier, whisks me quickly the ten or so miles to the stop on Columbia Road where the archive I want to visit today is situated. It is also close to the area Jessie knew.

I decide first to walk to the house on 6th Street up the steep hill from the Fraser River, where my research showed Jessie had lived and worked as a domestic, at least in 1913. My luck is in again, and although most of the old houses on this street have been demolished, No. 423 still stands.

It looks a well-kept detached house built of wood and slate, now split into three flats. It seems incongruous amongst the car parks and the retail lots nearby.

I go through the gate and start taking photos. Within a short time, a man who might be the owner arrives and catches me on his front lawn.

I am worried that he might protest and send me packing but when I describe my reason for being there, he is friendly and curious about a former resident of the house that he said his uncle had owned since the Second World War. He says that much has changed inside, as if to explain why he doesn't invite me in. I don't push my luck.

At his invitation, though, I go around the back and see that the house sits on a generous plot, with a vegetable patch to the rear. I notice a small grilled window at the apex of the roof under the gable, which could, I reckon, have allowed light into a small attic bedroom at one time. A servant's room, perhaps.

I offer to let the owner know if I discover any more about

the history of his house when I visit the archive later. It is the least I can do for my intrusion.

Instead of returning the way I came, I turn away from the main road, 6th Street, and one block away, find a leafier and more prosperous residential district with many lovingly preserved nineteenth and early twentieth-century houses – heritage houses, as they call them now – several with plaques.

I realise that Jessie's first residence was in the sort of area that she would have been reassured by. These are comfortable family homes, with trees and green space around them, like the better parts of Battersea and Victorian Cambridge.

I cannot help but conclude that there must have been some reason why she moved on from here so quickly. Maybe it was simply the determination to gain more independence than a life in service provided – or, more likely, it was connected with the arrival of the baby.

I walk back down the hill towards Columbia Road through a park, where I pause a while to collect my thoughts. I still know so little about the period between November 1912, when Jessie arrived in New Westminster, and March 1915, when her child was born.

The OPG confirmed that they had no birth record at all – and it seems their evidence for William's birth in the hospital in this city is based simply on an interview he had given as an old man to his carer. A line from that interview sticks with me: he told the carer that his mother, Jessie, had said the hospital was built by prisoners.

It seems such a random fact, if fact it is. I am hoping that the archive might be able to give me something more to go on than this.

I realise I am letting too much time go by. I get up and walk more briskly towards an old church with a spire – maybe Jessie worshipped here? – and break into a jog down the steep hill, soon returning to the jumble of more modern buildings on the Columbia Road.

One of the most recent – and much the most stylish – of these I find houses the New Westminster archive. I go up to the first floor and greet the archivist, who is presiding over an empty research room.

As I am his only customer, he grants me his sole attention. He brings out various old city records and maps for me to pore over, as well as a record that shows No. 423 on 6th was built in the 1890s. He also confirms to me that according to a local census of residents taken in 1908/9, a couple called Mr and Mrs Corbett, he an immigration officer, she a teacher, lived at the address. There is nothing more to confirm whether they were still living there four years later and employing Jessie.

Amongst the reference books on the shelf, I find a history of the Royal Columbian Hospital. I flick through it and find that yes, sure enough, a chain gang had helped in the construction of the original nineteenth-century hospital. It had been founded to provide medical care solely for the British garrison then based here. It was only in 1914 that there was a big expansion of the facilities, with a capacious new building, a separate maternity unit, isolation units for patients with contagious diseases, as well as nurses' accommodation.

So indeed William – born with what name exactly? – could have been one of the first babies delivered in the new hospital, but there is still so much about the circumstance of his birth that doesn't make sense to me.

I recall the OPG manager dismissing my question about the lack of a birth certificate by telling me it was not unusual for records from that period to just vanish, although his explanation – there were a lot of wooden buildings and a lot of fires – still fails to convince me.

Nor am I taken with the whole notion that Jessie, at the age of thirty-seven, a servant with just a few pounds in savings, recently arrived in a new country would have embarked on a liaison out of wedlock, risking a pregnancy and her precarious livelihood.

Or if she had actually married a man called Mac or McDonald, only to be widowed shortly afterwards, why is there no record of that either? I feel increasingly certain she assumed the name of her Bedfordshire cousin – also a common name in her new country.

Yes, as a servant she could have been vulnerable to sexual assault – yes, that is certainly plausible, I know. Maybe, with what we know now, the most plausible scenario of all. Yet, sitting reading this book about the hospital plants another idea in my head.

Could Jessie have worked as a children's nurse at the hospital? She had a lot of experience, if not any formal qualifications, but by 1915 they might have been grateful for her to work there in some capacity, to fill the gaps created by the nurses recruited for the field hospitals in Belgium. Surely someone who worked at the hospital would be more likely to know the story of the chain gang.

My thoughts go further: what if Jessie got a baby in the

same way as Hattie Rooke, her own adoptive mother?

After a couple of hours, I exhaust the resources here. I thank the archivist for his time and attention – I have remained his only customer this morning.

As I leave, I ask him one last question: where was the original New Westminster station, the one that Jessie would have arrived at after her long journey from Quebec and the place from which she might have left for Vancouver?

He takes me to the window and points straight across the road to a long brick building with arches. That was the old station, he says confidently. Right there.

I see Cousin Jessie now, coming alone with her journey-battered suitcase. Then I see her leaving, again with that suitcase, but now with an even more precious bundle – a baby. A baby in a shawl, hidden from view, still shrouded in mystery a century on.

As I take the Skytrain back to Vancouver, I have time to return to the iPad and read that interview between the carer and the aged William that OPG had retained. The file contains notes taken from two such interviews, one typed, one handwritten.

The carer, it is clear from this, had been urged by the OPG officials who had already taken William into care to find out what they could about any family he might have. As I read her notes, I notice something odd.

I zoom in and discover something easily missed with the naked eye. The handwritten transcript refers to Jessie as William's 'mother'. Yes, with the benefit of the zoom, I see there are clearly inverted commas around the word.

Why would you put 'mother' in inverted commas unless

there was some doubt about the matter? Maybe the OPG had never noticed these two little marks, or had, but discounted the possibility that Jessie was not William's birth mother.

It was most unlikely that the early heir hunters, Ian Hilder of Lewes amongst them, would have seen this document. Even if they had, the picture they'd painted of Jessie as a woman of doubtful credibility, who hadn't thought twice about falsifying her date of birth on an immigration record and made up details of her parentage on a solemn certificate of marriage, would be all of a piece with someone who'd have an illegitimate child.

It was not of a piece, though, with the Cousin Jessie I feel I know – and I am confident now I know her rather better than they did.

Maybe the opportunity to have a child of her own presented itself to her in the maternity ward at the Royal Columbian Hospital. Hattie Rooke, the childless widow, had been forty-one when the young Bedfordshire couple who came to Cambridge to have their baby came across someone who would love their daughter and, with some financial support, bring her up. Jessie was just three years younger when Willie came into the world.

So it's not impossible, surely, that rather than giving birth to the boy herself, she might have helped out another mother, just as Hattie had done. Jessie loved babies – she'd kept all the photos of those she had nursed in Cambridge, hadn't she?

With her fertility fast declining, might she not have seized any opportunity to have a child of her own? A child whose birth record could indeed have been consumed by fire, but perhaps deliberately cast by his new mother into the flames of a domestic hearth.

Then, the boy's new identity could have been assumed simply with a new name written into a birthday book. Was this, I wonder, any less plausible than a birth certificate destroyed in a mysterious blaze in a wooden building?

My day in New Westminster has taken me in a direction I never expected. Following in her footsteps can surely get me even closer to the truth of her life over the coming week. One last day in Vancouver – and then I am heading prairie-ward , well what used to be prairie that is – to try to solve the mystery of how Mrs McDonald became a farmer's wife.

Chapter Nine

Vancouver, 2017

The farmer wants a wife and the wife wants a child but not in that order, it seemed.

Jessie got a child and created not one but two new identities – was that how it was? – the truth never to be fully recovered, blanketed by the fog of history? I am standing and musing on a suspension bridge in a park in North Vancouver, the distant view obscured by smoke.

Don't look down – look at the camera.

A couple of Canadian friends have offered to show me more of the sights and capture me on the bridge as if alone. The pall from the forest fires hangs increasingly heavily over Vancouver, covering the city in a stiflingly hot cloak. In Capilano Park, we can find relief from the heat among the towering redwoods; trees which dwarf us, standing proudly here for hundreds of years and which we know will outlive us all.

My thoughts never stray far from Cousin Jessie. I read the information board by the suspension bridge and see that this place has attracted visitors since the nineteenth-century wood and rope bridge was replaced with a sturdier wire cable one in 1910. Jessie could have walked and gasped at the views over the tree-lined canyon as I am doing now.

Don't look down – she might have been told that here too – but for her, the more important imperative surely was – don't look back. If she came to this city with the infant Willie, she had to look to his future now, not just to her own.

I'm more certain now that she did move here with her baby boy. As well as that street directory entry, I had discovered in England, of a 'Mrs Jessie McDonald, widow' living here, I now have the confirmation from the letter I had seen in the OPG, the account by Mrs Kerr, which stated that the couple came from Vancouver. I am sure that she would have known the difference between this city and New Westminster, even though the once two distinct settlements had now been enveloped into Greater Vancouver.

I haven't got any further than that street directory in finding any further trace of this 'widow' McDonald living on the East side of the city. Trying to exhaust every avenue to find her, I go through telephone directories from that era in the library, but it's hardly a surprise she isn't listed there. I suppose she could not have afforded such a new-fangled thing – and who was going to call her, anyway?

Later, I visit that one place she might have lived at No. 1840, 7th Avenue East and find a neat, gabled, two-storied brick house, in a tree-lined street not unlike the house in New Westminster. It is in what is known as the Grandview district of the city. This area which was on the interurban streetcar route between New Westminster and Vancouver, started to boom in the early years of the twentieth century with all sorts of shops and businesses as well as housing, all clustered around Commercial Drive.

7th Avenue is bathed in a twilight glow when I arrive and looks even now the sort of neighbourhood which Jessie could have judged respectable, with cheaper housing to rent than on the west side and plenty of opportunities to find work. Still, I know she didn't stay here long, three, four years at most.

Shortly after the end of the First World War she took her boy with her to a place, geographically only twenty miles or so distant, but in character, a world away. A city girl made a move to the country. Why?

I knew that by 1919, many of the jobs women had been doing were handed back to the men as they returned from the war. This so-called Great War, although it had taken place half a world away, disrupted lives here too; taking thousands of men away to fight for the British Empire, many never to return. The women had to cope on their own, doing work they had never been called on to do before.

Maybe life was just too much of a struggle for Jessie in Vancouver or maybe the city air did not suit the boy. I knew that there were regular recruitment drives in Canada to encourage people to leave the cities and populate other parts of the Federation, advertising sunshine and golden corn and happy families bathed in the warm glow of prosperity. Didn't I know the lure of the countryside myself – moving as I did with our family out of London in the hope of a better life more than twenty years ago?

Why again, though, would an elderly farmer advertise for a housekeeper in the city rather than ask a local woman to help him? A librarian checked for me and couldn't find anything other than local jobs being advertised.

Maybe Jessie met someone by chance who told her about Langley Prairie and the number of men living alone in rural places like this. Maybe Jessie just took a chance and got on a train one day, keeping going till she had left the city well behind.

It's all conjecture though. I can find no answer to this mystery here. I know I am missing something but it eludes me right now.

It is my last day here, as tomorrow I am setting off for the Vancouver suburb of Langley, taking the same journey as Jessie did from the city. As I stand in the twilight, I feel close to my cousin again.

I can glimpse her ghost under the street lights. I see her leaving, with her increasingly battered case, holding her small boy Willie firmly by the hand as she sets off again with another one-way ticket. Hoping still, surely, for that elusive new life, this time on Langley Prairie, Mrs McDonald would soon with this move assume another new identity.

I knew about that too.

Leicester, 1968

The summer of 1968 already seems to have lost the magic of '67. Instead it is proving quite unsettling. Just when teachers want us to stay really calm, with our first proper exams, our O levels, underway, instead it's the most disturbing time I can remember.

Sixth formers, who are allowed sometimes to listen to the radio tell us Fifth Formers that there's terrible news from America on the lunchtime bulletin. Another Kennedy, almost as popular and glamorous as his brother, has been assassinated.

Bobby was running for President and it seems he's been killed on the campaign trail. A suspect has been arrested at the scene in Los Angeles. This news comes only a couple of months after the civil rights leader Martin Luther King also met an untimely death in Memphis.

Shocking as that was, it didn't compare, for me at least, with another shock I'd had over the Easter holidays. Quite suddenly after nearly ten years we moved house and Dad left his job at the club.

I'm not told very much about why or where we are going. I'm not sure whether Mum and Dad have known for a while and told me nothing until the holiday or whether it was a sudden decision, made whether voluntarily or involuntarily I don't know. Mum says that we'll be going somewhere better – by that, it seems, she means we'll be going to a better part of town, somewhere like Knighton or Stoneygate.

I have no memory at all of the removal vans coming. I can't even remember whether I packed up my own possessions: my Beatles collection, my books, the globe, yes and the childish things I still clung to – the glass animals, the dolls and the teddy bears. Maybe I took the most precious of these in the case I used for my holidays rather than entrust them to the removal men.

Our furniture must have gone into storage as we did not move straightaway into a new place. Instead, we went first to a small hotel on the London Road. We weren't there for more than a week or two and then we moved into our new home.

It is a semi-detached house in Knighton. I knew at once it would be a great improvement on the house by the club. For one thing, it has a pretty garden with a proper lawn and flower beds.

It's quieter too, although I miss the regular rumble of the trains at first. I remember the landlord came around to check we were ok and to give Dad the rent book. Yes, whatever this move was occasioned by, it's not going to make life easier for Mum and Dad to make ends meet.

Mum tells me that she's going to have to go back to work to help pay the bills. She is going to brush up her shorthand and her typing skills, last used in earnest before I was born. She's hoping to get an office job.

I think she's quite guilty about going back to work but I don't mind at all. I will have a lot more time to myself in the house, especially in the school holidays, and can make my own lunch. I also think it will be a good thing for Mum too – get her out of the house at last.

As for Dad, he's retraining to be a bus driver. He proudly shows us his new public service vehicle licence when he qualifies. He'll still be working shifts: early mornings, weekends and late nights are involved but that's nothing new of course.

It only takes a few weeks for Mum to find a job too. She'll be working as a secretary to Mr Francis who is the boss of a small textile firm based just walking distance away. Apparently, Mum and Mr Francis knew each other when they were at school. He's clearly done well for himself in the intervening years. Mum has to buy new and smarter clothes for the job and when I see her leaving the house for the first time, I see almost a new woman.

So, shocking as the move was to me at first, I have no doubt that it has been a good thing. Shame, though, there's not going to be a summer holiday this year, but never mind. I can get to know the neighbourhood.

The streets nearby are quiet and leafy and there is a pleasant park to wander in too. I can also walk to the lido when the weather is warm enough to swim outdoors. When it rains, I can listen in peace to the radio or to my records.

It's a shame there's no new Beatles LP this summer to buy. There are rumours of arguments in the recording studio and that John's girlfriend, Yoko Ono, who shows up there on a regular basis, is driving him away from Paul. He's got a new girlfriend too, an American photographer called Linda Eastman, and George spends more and more time in India, with the gurus. They stopped touring ages ago now, but I can't imagine them splitting up.

Now, that really would be disturbing.

Cloverdale, B.C, 2017

Would the bus ride from the end of the Skyline train taking me to Langley never end?

Maybe there was an express bus that I missed but this stopping route which has wound through residential areas, shopping malls and industrial estates takes me a full one and half hours. I appear to be the only tourist on the bus, which isn't surprising as Langley is well off the main tourist track.

I sit with my wheelie suitcase, my rucksack and my handbag packed in close by me and try in vain to recognise any landmarks outside the window. The strange cloud, which is in fact the smoke from the ever-closer forest fires, obscures the sun making the journey even more disorientating.

It's an old-fashioned bus with no digital signage to help me identify the stops. I am cursing the false economy of not having paid for data on my phone so that I can follow my progress via the mobile satnav. Instead, I open my pocket street atlas of Greater Vancouver to make some attempt to follow where I am going.

I am certainly now on the South side of the Fraser River, travelling in a South-East direction, the best part of twenty miles from downtown Vancouver. I'm winding my way through the suburbs of Surrey (which don't look one bit like the prosperous county I know to the South West of London), via Cloverdale (which sounds pastoral but isn't) and hoping to end up in Langley City, the terminus of this route.

As we get close to my destination, I start to look out for one of the addresses I know was Cousin Jessie's: the one she called on the back of a photograph taken in the 1920s, '*R.R. No 2 Langley Prairie, ¾ mile S.W. of P.O on Rd to Cloverdayl.*' Over the best part of a century, this area has not only been re-named but transformed. Might this be, I wonder, the address now known more succinctly as No.19799, 56th Avenue, Langley City?

We must be close now to my stop – and maybe to this very

address, I reckon, as I spot a sign marking the junction of 196 Street and 56th. As I peer out the window to try to see further along 56th, we take a detour around an industrial estate, completely confusing me again, before emerging finally at what the driver tells me is the best stop to find a cab to take me to my B-and-B. I am not going to risk a long walk weighed down with luggage on a hot and humid lunchtime.

I alight from the bus alone, complete with my wheelie and all to find myself near a small mall opposite the Greyhound station. My anxious gaze takes in a discount store, apparently with no customers, a billboard for the Cascades casino, a small parking lot, but not a single cab. I feel well and truly lost now but at last someone comes around the corner and advises me to stay put, as she assures me a taxi will come along soon.

After a few more anxious minutes alone, along comes a cab. I hail it and within a ten-minute ride back in the direction from which I have come, I find my destination in a pleasant and quiet residential road quite different in ambience from the route the bus took. I wheel my case round to the back as directed and ring the bell. My host, Lorna, welcomes me warmly and ushers me inside.

It is a comfortable family home, traditionally furnished, where I will be able to relax when I am not out and about on my research. After a cup of tea and a short rest, I feel re-energised. I am up for a walk around.

I need to buy something for my supper and I ask Lorna where I can find a shop. Yes, there's a small mall nearby, but she says it will take half an hour to walk there. Am I sure about that?

I realise that the old British habit of walking to the shops has almost died out on this side of the Atlantic. Lorna gives me directions to take me on a walking route away from the main highway and tells me that as well as the mall, I can find a library, the local archive – and a good cup of coffee too. What more could this traveller want?

I set off and after a pleasant walk in the hazy mid-afternoon sunshine, I find myself back at the 56th but well to the West of the 196th block I will hope to find another day. I can see the library and archive building on the other side of the road.

It is not so easy to see how I get there. Huge trucks rattle by as well as a steady stream of cars, so there is no way I am going to be able to cross at this point. I look to my left and can see some traffic lights a couple of hundred metres away. Above the highway, green signs point left to the American border, right towards Highway 1 otherwise known as the Trans-Canada Highway, and straight ahead to Vancouver International airport and to the ferry port at Nanaimo, the crossing point to Vancouver Island. No wonder it is busy.

I cross the road at the lights and make my way back towards the library. It turns out that this has a thriving family history section, which should come in useful for me. I have only booked to stay in the area for five days, until Tuesday, so I note with surprise and pleasure that the library is not only open on Saturday but on Sundays as well: opening hours which are unheard of in England, at any time, and even more so now in the age of austerity. There will be no wasted time for me over these next few days.

In the archive next door, I inquire whether they have any

records for Langley here – no, I am told this place holds only the records for the next-door municipality of Surrey. Still, the helpful archivist (they are all invariably so on my visit) suggests some old maps and photographs I might be interested in.

I sit down at a desk to look at them. There is one captioned 'Land clearing on Langley Prairie' undated but which could have been taken as late as 1910 even though there is an ox pulling the cart in the picture.

Another, of an archaic looking steam-driven threshing machine, dated to 1920, shows that some primitive mechanisation had arrived. A picture of the Cloverdale Post Office, dated to the 1920s, shows two cars parked outside. Change was clearly accelerating as Jessie arrived.

After a short stay here, I leave the archive and walk in the other direction from the highway where I am told I'll find a café. It is housed in one of several heritage buildings as they call them round here.

These have managed to be preserved from the bulldozer, reminding the residents and passers-by of the rural settlement that was here before the highways came. This was the 'Cloverdayl' which Jessie would have known.

Alongside the street, there are several sculptures, erected in commemoration of the men they call the pioneers. One statue looks to my eyes like an American cowboy, the other a timeless figure of a labourer in tee-shirt and denim. They are fine images of the working men, the colonists, who had hewn farms, roads and factories from the wilderness, but what a shame that there are no women commemorated here, let alone any reference to the people of the First Nations. Surely the immigrant women were as much a part of that story, even if not so muscular in their achievements?

I think of George Underwood, the farmer, who gave Jessie a housekeeping job and who would become her husband. Now, he was a pioneer alright.

I'd found his name in a British Columbia directory, farming in Langley Prairie as early as 1882. This was one of the oldest white-settled places in British Columbia, indeed in the whole of Canada.

The Hudson's Bay Trading Company had come here first. They'd started by trading goods from their fortified compound with the people of the First Nations. Then they had diversified into farming, clearing and claiming the forest inland from the Fraser River.

In 1858 gold had been discovered and the fort had become important as a supply station for miners heading to the gold fields. By the 1880s the gold rush had ended and Fort Langley had begun to decline. The Hudson's Bay company decided to carve out one hundred-acre plots from the lands they had claimed to the new farmers arriving into the area mainly from England, Scotland and Ireland. It was good fertile loam with clay subsoil, potentially another sort of goldmine.

George Underwood was one of the purchasers. Originally from the Borders area between Scotland and England, he had come to British Columbia in his thirties, having taken his chance when times for farmers in Britain were particularly tough. He followed in the footsteps of his older brother Peter, who took a different road, into the vastness of the Northern territories, settling there with his British wife.

The bachelor George went to the less forbidding West

Coast to seek his fortune. I reckon he would have been delighted by the fertility and relatively mild climate of the Fraser Valley, quite a change from the often cold, wet and difficult terrain of the Cumberland and Dumfriesshire he'd farmed before.

I looked up on my tablet the description I'd found of Langley Prairie in the 1882 Directory. As I sit in the café now almost within earshot of the rumbling trucks on the 56th highway, I read it again.

The anonymous writer talked of the area's remoteness but also of its many attractive qualities – including the two rivers flowing through the area, the Salmon and the Nicomeki – 'both abound in trout, large and delicious'.

It talked of its timberlands, both the 'pine and cedar giants of bygone ages and a dense covering of bush, pine and vine maple'. The prairie 'affords excellent pasture for their stock, large quantities of prairie hay are also gathered. These flats present excellent inducements to the huntsman and are largely visited in the season by sportsmen from the cities in quest of game... the neighbouring woods team with grouse... and the rivers with duck.'

The author's next sentence reminds me that some things here don't change.

'In dry seasons fires have travelled almost throughout the district, making fearful havoc of the forest trees and leaving only blackened and ungainly stumps. In many places, only here and there a tall pine or cedar stands uninjured, having escaped the conflagrations, at the same time each lot contains abundant material for the purposes of fencing, building, and also for fuel.'

I sip my coffee, thinking nervously of that threatening cloud on the horizon and carry on.

'Beside the Hudson Bay Company's Farm there are upwards of a thousand acres of prairie land adjacent to it on the west side. This land is … at the present moment bearing luxuriant crops of wheat and oats. Returning from the prairie to the Fort by the road, the scenery is truly charming. There is Mount Baker, in Washington Territory, away in the background to the right, rearing his hoary head high above the intervening country and looking down from his lofty seat in calm and dignified composure upon the scene beneath…'

I wonder whether I'll ever get to see Mount Baker, a landmark close to the Canadian border normally viewable for miles around.

'Along the road on either side there is a richness of verdure, a wealth and profusion of vegetation seldom equalled, and indicative of soil of extraordinary fertility… a series of bush farms, which show what intelligence and patient industry can accomplish in reclaiming bush land. Most of the occupants of these farms came here with little or no capital five or six years ago. Single handed they have now 15, 20 and 30 acres under crop this season – have comfortable homes – have oxen, cows, hogs, fowls and are free of debt.'

The author of the directory has not done yet.

'The soil and climate of this district are especially adapted to the cultivation of hay, roots, and the common kinds of fruit, as apples, pears, plums, cherries, currants etc. The climate is mild and salubrious, greatly resembling that of the South of England and the North West departments of France.'

No wonder a young Scottish farmer travelled thousands of miles over sea and land to take his chance here. George was one of seventy-six farmers listed in that directory, with only a handful of other occupations mentioned: a fish foreman, a saw mill and flour mill proprietor, a store keeper and postmaster (one man, two jobs), a school teacher and a Presbyterian minister, the Reverend Alexander Dunn, ministering to the farmers many of whom were of Scottish stock, like George. It was a sturdy and stoic community, no doubt.

By the time Cousin Jessie arrived here, George had grown old and the community had adopted a new name, Milner. As well as the railway lines, electric pylons strode across the land. Still, the scene then was much closer to that 1882 one, than the twenty-first century one I am looking out on now.

Refreshed by the coffee, I set out for the mall to pick up the ingredients for my supper. I have to hazard a second crossing of the highway to get there before walking the half hour back to the B-and-B. It is a beautiful early September evening, and I relax, at least for a while.

I know it will be a busy day and maybe the most crucial of my trip tomorrow. In my bedroom, I work out what I am going to take with me for my trip to Fort Langley.

I have made an appointment to see the archivist there who says she can provide me with some interesting information. I've brought just a few of the photos from Jessie's collection with me to show her: ones which seem to have been taken in Milner. These residents look in an altogether more prosperous situation than that of the Jessie and William I have pictured in front of a shack.

There is also one which I'm pretty sure is of George Underwood. It is a black and white print pasted on a large piece of cardboard. An old man is standing in front of a large well-built, two-storied farmhouse with a veranda and a rambling rose bush by the steps up to the front door.

George is posing for a cameraman who must have been standing some way from him to take in all the house in his picture. George is too far away from the camera to make out his expression but you can see he is wearing his work clothes: a white collarless shirt with long sleeves, braces and dark, slightly baggy trousers. He seems to have some sort of headband keeping his mane of white hair in place. He clearly had not made any effort to smarten himself up for the photograph.

If this is George, then this house is on the main road leading from Langley up towards the fort, and the one I will take tomorrow. Trunk Road, it was called, at the time Jessie shared this house with him. This is the road the Directory writer called 'charming' and with a 'wealth and profusion of vegetation'.

Looking at this photograph, it was clear that such an old man might be in want of a woman to keep such a place clean and tidy. Jessie certainly had the qualifications to do the job.

Still, it remained an unlikely tale how they had come to meet and to marry. Maybe I will unlock that mystery in the coming few days.

I settle myself to sleep, in anticipation of my own journey tomorrow to the place Jessie called, at least for a few years, home – in anticipation, but also with some trepidation.

I've also got an appointment at the Fort Langley cemetery

and I will be visiting three graves there tomorrow: George Underwood's, that of William, who took his name – and Cousin Jessie's.

Chapter Ten

Langley, B.C, September 2017

I have woken early again. I'm thinking about whether I've got Jessie all wrong.

That letter has come to the forefront of my waking mind: the one from Mrs Velma Kerr about Jessie and William's arrival in Milner nearly a century ago. There's something troubling me about her account, more than the bare words.

I read it again:

'When a young child I lived with my family on a farm in Milner ajoining(sic) the farm of the late George Underwood.

Mr. Underwood was a rather elderly batchelor (sic) who had lived on that farm for many years. One day a lady arrived on his farm with her young son who was about five years old. Her name was Mrs McDonald and her son's name was Willie. They came from Vancouver. Mrs McDonald remained to be Mr. Underwood's housekeeper. Willie went to school for several years in Milner. Mr. Underwood became old and shortly before he died Mrs McDonald had the minister for the local church come to the house to marry her and Mr Underwood…

It was no secret that Willie was an illegitimate child...

Willie and his mother lived together in a small home in Langley City after leaving the farm after Mr Underwood died.

They made few friends.'

I know one thing that's troubling me: the timeline of her story can't be right. It reads as if the story of George and Jessie takes place over quite a length of time. In reality, it spanned just two years at most.

Mrs McDonald arrives with a child of 'about five', she says; maybe that was an easy miscalculation. I reckon he was four and it was sometime in 1919 when they arrived.

Mrs Kerr says that Mrs McDonald 'remained' to be George's housekeeper and that Willie went to school for several years. Mr Underwood 'became old' (he was already seventy-five in 1919) and 'shortly before he died' Mrs McDonald had the minister come to marry them. The marriage took place in July 1920 and George Underwood died the following March so it was hardly a deathbed wedding.

Willie was just turned six when his stepfather died. I look now at his school photograph that I have brought with me, one of the more minor treasures in Cousin Jessie's box. He is in the back row of a line-up, one of the oldest of the children there. It looks like it was taken when he was about ten or eleven, around 1925/6, long after the farmer's death. The pencilled address on the back, in Jessie's hand, is of that of the *'small home in Langley City'* on the road to *'Cloverdayl'*.

The more I weigh up what I know, the hard evidence I have, the more I find Mrs Kerr's account confused and alternately stretched and telescoped. As far as the OPG was concerned, the key evidence in her letter, Exhibit K, presented to the Supreme Court, is that William Underwood was born before Jessie met George. (I recall how categoric Mrs Jenkins had been that George was not the biological father of William even though I do not believe any DNA testing was done.)

The second key point for them was Mrs Kerr's assurance: *'It was no secret that Willie was an illegitimate child.'*

It is this line though that troubles me the most but for a different reason. There is something quietly damning or at least disdainful in this sentence – that along with the final line: *'They made few friends.'*

There is, I am thinking, an underlying narrative here, suggested by that phrasing of *'shortly before he died Mrs McDonald had the minister for the local church come to the house to marry her and Mr. Underwood.'* It's that *'had the minister'* which surely has a whiff of disapproval in it as well as putting the death of the farmer in the same sentence as if the two events were linked.

Could a young child have known all this and have remembered the story in this way? Surely it was a more adult account, perhaps revealing a prevailing and persistent view in a small community: of a stranger who comes from the city into a village with a child of uncertain paternity in tow and who manipulates a frail old man first into giving her a housekeeper's job and then just before he dies inveigles him into marrying her.

Then, again, how was it '*no secret*' that the child was illegitimate?

Would Jessie have been shouting it from the rooftops? – hardly. On her marriage certificate, she describes herself as the widow McDonald. The child could have been legitimate.

Would George have talked about it? –again, unlikely. He'd taken in the boy, after all, it would seem quite happily and had surely got better things to do than gossip about his new housekeeper's private life or complain about her immorality.

It's possible of course that Jessie had shared her secret with someone – revealed that she had taken into her care another woman's child – as I had concluded from my day in New Westminster was the most plausible scenario. Indeed, she might have told George – and the word had got out.

Mrs Kerr did not claim to have known William in recent years, although her address is given as one in Langley City. She does though refer to the names and addresses of two women, who at the time she wrote, in 1995, were also living in the area and who she said were '*related to George Underwood in some way*'. One of these had Underwood in her name.

I have some reason to think that the Underwood family may have shared Mrs Kerr's view of Jessie and her child. As well as photographs of George's side of the family left safely in my box file at home, I have two letters from George's Scottish sister, Margaret, written to Jessie shortly after George's death.

These had troubled me too ever since I had read them

when I had first gone through the contents of the box of memorabilia. Jessie had kept these letters neatly together in a single small buff-coloured envelope. They were addressed to her as Mrs Jessie Underwood, Langley Prairie, British Columbia.

The first, dated November 24th, and I reckon written in 1921, was friendly enough and was clearly in response to a letter from Jessie. Mrs Bell is concerned that '*it will be lonely for your two selves*' on the farm. She wishes that '*everything was squared up better for everyone. I hope it will be soon.*' She also refers to a photo that Jessie had sent her.

'*You are strong looking but you will be changed now. It must be a long time taken by the make of your dress and as I promised I am sending it back. The little boy might be pleased to see it years after this.*'

I am sure that the photo which Jessie must have sent – and which Mrs Bell returned – is the small *carte de visite* taken in a Cambridge studio when Jessie was a very young woman and working as a nanny. Inscribed on the back, in Jessie's hand, is her signature, Mrs J. Underwood, not Heading, as she had been when it was taken the best part of twenty years earlier.

Margaret Bell continues wistfully:

'*Many a time I remember poor old George and wonder what he was like. Had I been younger I would have come to see his place. I have the photo of his house and it looks well.*'

No doubt that was a reference to the picture of George standing by his farmhouse door. I have learnt that itinerant photographers used to travel around the countryside taking pictures of the settlers to show off their new places – and so their success – to family back home.

Mrs Bell also has a question and a suggestion for Jessie.

'What part of this country do you belong to? You might easily come back to your native place if you have friends.'

For sure, Mrs Bell had no idea that Jessie had booked a one-way ticket when she had emigrated. She ends the letter warmly.

'I hope you will write soon again and say how you are and the boy. I am Sincerely Yours, Maggie Bell.'

The second letter was shorter and altogether sharper. This was dated February 16, 1922 and received according to the postmark in Langley Prairie in early March.

'I was much astonished at the contents of your last letter. I knew my brother George much better than ever you did and am quite sure it was never his wish or desire for a strange man's boy or a woman's either to possess his farm.

You wrote out a will leaving it to you but it was of no use and you know that. You were going to leave him if he did not marry you, a poor old alone man of 77 or 78.

How sorry I am when I remember him now. That some of his own friends was (sic) not there to look after him.

*However, he is where there is no sorrow or suffering now
and I know he would long for some of his own people.'*

This time there are no warm wishes for Jessie and her boy
and no invitation to write again. No more Maggie either, but
signed simply, *M. Bell.*

This surely is all of a piece with that same narrative given
by Mrs Kerr. A woman, who was from the servant class, with
a '*strange man's boy*' takes advantage of a frail old man, by
threatening to abandon him, if he does not marry her, then
concocts a will leaving his substantial property to her.

As I think about this angry letter now, I also wonder if
Jessie had confided to the older woman, who was now her
sister-in-law after all, in an earlier letter how William had
been born and how and why they had come together to
George's home from Vancouver. Mrs Bell's taunt: '*it was never
his wish or desire for a strange man's boy or a woman's either to
possess his farm.*' is ambiguous as to which strange woman she
is referring to.

Cousin Jessie – or William's real mother?

Of course, Jessie's letter which had caused such outrage is
lost for ever. How I wish I had it now!

As it is, I have in that letter the depiction of a gold-digger:
a woman of suspicion indeed. Can I believe this? Do I want
to believe this?

Before I set off for Fort Langley, which I hope will help me
build a kinder narrative, I think back to a trip I made just a
month ago. I went to find out more about Cousin Jessie's
correspondent and possible nemesis.

The Scottish Borders, August 2017

I am driving the two hundred and fifty miles from Cambridge to Cumbria in search of the childhood home of George Underwood. I know from my online search it is in a remote area very close to the border with Scotland.

Reaching the house of a friend who lives not far away around tea time, after a short stop for refreshment, she offers to drive me there that same evening. I am pleased to accept her offer, as she is familiar with the area and I will be able to concentrate on taking in the landscape after a long day at the wheel.

We go a couple of junctions north on the M6, then on past Carlisle passing the point where the Romans had marked the border with Hadrian's Wall. Then we turn onto the A road to Longtown. This is the last of the market towns of North West England before the border; a town which had found a fame of sorts, during the foot and mouth crisis of 2001, when the first sheep found with that dread disease had been purchased at the market here.

I have never been here before, but I know that Mrs Margaret Bell had. Amongst the Underwood mementoes and photographs, I now own, there is a colour postcard of the blacksmith's shop at Gretna Green, with a Dumfries postmark of 2p.m., August 27, 1908. This is addressed simply to Mr Underwood, Langley, New Westminster, British Columbia, Canada. This had clearly been sufficient to reach its intended recipient.

It was signed simply M.B and started '*Was at Longtown last week.*'

I have a photograph of George's older sister, which I have brought with me on this expedition. It was taken in Moryson's photographic studio in Dumfries, around the same time as the postcard.

Here sits a confident elderly woman looking directly at the camera with a fearless gaze. She wears a good-quality suit in the Edwardian style, a ruched and patterned blouse, with a laced edging to the high neck and a brooch at the throat, softening the severity of the plain jacket and long skirt. A long gold chain around her neck almost reaches her lap and on her left hand, lying gently over her right, are three rings, including a wedding band. She looks to be a woman of substance.

My online research suggested that Mrs Margaret Ewart Bell could have been the linchpin of this farming family. She stayed in Scotland, while several of her siblings, nephews and nieces, moved away to far-flung parts of the British Empire. As well as her brothers, George and Peter who travelled to Canada, another brother, John, served in Hong Kong. Her sister Ann's children, George and Mary Underwood Walker, also made their lives abroad, working in India, South Africa, and finally, by 1914 ended up in Washington State, close to the Canadian border.

There is an immigration document in the Canadian archive I have found, showing that Mary Underwood Walker had entered British Columbia on a temporary visa in that year. No doubt she would have wished to visit her uncle George in Milner. She gave the authorities the name of Mrs Bell as a reference. No doubt the older woman had encouraged this visit to see how her brother, then entering his eighth decade, was faring alone on his farm. This was of course a few years before Jessie arrived on his doorstep.

Leaving Longtown, we are driving now on a small country road, towards the place where George and Margaret started out on their lives of imperial endeavour. We weave our way close to the River Esk which marks the border between England and Scotland, some ten miles through quiet and peaceful terrain.

At last we come to Nichol Forest and its ancient church, the place they were baptised. It is built of local stone, small and sturdy, like its nineteenth-century congregation no doubt and topped by a slim slate-topped spire. We stop a while and walk through the churchyard in the still grey summer evening.

Then we move on again, up into the still remoter countryside, in search of Nookfoot farm. We go down ever more winding and narrow lanes, going gradually up hill, past the Old Hall, until we find what we think might be the Underwood family farm at last.

We haven't passed a single vehicle nor seen a soul. We park the car and walk through the gate not expecting to find anyone. There was no sign of life initially, no cattle in the byres, nor sheep in the fields, then someone emerges from one of the cottages to confirm that we had reached our goal. This was Nookfoot indeed; no doubt a bustling working farm in the mid-nineteenth century but still as remote and isolated then as it is now. Such a place would have made both George and Margaret equally tough and self-reliant, I reckon.

The following day, I set off alone to find Margaret's home after she married, across the border in Dumfriesshire – a little place called Stepford, from which she had written to Jessie. My first stop was the market town of Dumfries.

I haven't been here I realise for forty-five years when I had a student summer job in these parts. I worked as a sort of companion and factotum for an elderly woman who lived close by. I remember Mum and Dad hadn't approved at all; they didn't like me doing what they saw as menial work, even on a temporary basis.

Now before me, I find a scene which is familiar to me; not from my own memory but from another one of Mrs Bell's cards to George. This one is more than twice the size of a normal postcard and made of much stiffer cardboard. Sent by halfpenny packet post, it bore the postmark 'Auldgirth, July 31, 1909'. On the face of the card is a photograph of Dumfries High Street looking towards the clock tower. There is a tear and mark at the top centre of the card, such as a drawing pin might have left. I wonder if it had once been pinned on George's wall.

I pay a visit to the local family history group who have a shop in the town. From them, I find out where I need to go to find Mrs Bell's home in Stepford, which is just a few miles from Auldgirth, as well as the churchyard where she was buried. I am delighted – research which could have taken me hours on my own on the internet, I complete with their help in no time at all here. I have time to take a break for lunch before setting off again.

So it's the afternoon when I find myself on another long and winding road, and then standing outside an imposing house, set proudly above the valley, about ten miles from Dumfries. I decide to take a chance and knock on the door.

I am in luck – someone is in. I explain my mission and I am invited in for a cup of tea. I am fortunate that the current owners are interested in the history of the house and its former residents.

They show me a photo of the farmhouse and the nearby railway halt, a long-closed station, both taken around the time Mrs Bell lived there. Indeed, Mrs Bell's husband John had sold some of his land to the railway company. In return, I give them my picture of her for them to photocopy.

While this is done, I stand close to the bow window of the front parlour looking down over the valley and Cairn Water. It is a lovely view, particularly on a sunny summer afternoon.

Maybe the widowed Mrs Bell sat in this very spot to write her letters to Jessie. Maybe her anger exploded in this very room as she read Jessie's replies.

As I take in the scene, I think about how a woman like Margaret Bell would have regarded the claims of someone like Jessie. From her photograph, Jessie presented as a shy Victorian-era servant. It was unthinkable to Mrs Bell surely, that such a woman could take on her family's farm.

It was man's work for a true Underwood, she would have judged, this one hundred acres of the British Empire. After all, it had been first claimed as such by the Hudson's Bay trading company a century before and its now imperial soil had been nurtured by the colonist George for more than thirty years.

How dare an uppity servant, who'd somehow weaselled her way into the place, think she could grab it for herself and her illegitimate boy! I see the Edwardian matron at this window now quietly fuming.

I can well imagine her firing up her nephew and niece, George and Mary, to get on the case. Jessie was only the housekeeper, a boarder at best – and with a bastard son to boot – not proper family, not even proper. Get her out!

I turn back from the window as my unexpected host has returned with Mrs Bell's portrait now copied. I am soon on the road again.

About five miles away, I find a churchyard in a place called Holywood – a wee place as different from its American namesake as you could imagine. The local historian I met in Dumfries has told me Mrs Bell is buried here and has given me the plot number.

I walk through the silent graveyard and it is not long before I am standing in front of the headstone of one John Bell, with this inscription under it: '*also Margaret Underwood, his wife, who died 29th June 1923.*'

She survived her Canadian brother by only two years. She would have gone to her eternal rest, knowing for sure that the farm her brother had bought and nurtured was staying in the family – a family which did not embrace an English housekeeper and her 'strange man's boy'.

Langley, September, 2017

As I call to mind that Scottish trip and a grave carved out of granite in memory of an adamantine woman, I think of another one I will stand before later today. Jessie's dream, if dream it was, of building a life for herself and her child on their own farm in Langley Prairie surely would not have survived contact with the tough reality, even if a woman thousands of miles away hadn't set herself against her.

Still she did leave another property to her son, didn't she? Her dream – that very American if now contested dream – didn't die at the first encounter with opposition, did it?

Time to get on with the day now, I tell myself. I have an important appointment in just a couple of hours to keep. I must get dressed quickly and go down to breakfast with Lorna.

Leicester, 1969

I can't remember there ever being anything on the television at breakfast time before but this morning is special. I am sitting watching pictures of a man on the moon, in a space suit, walking down a ladder, and you can just about catch what he says through the crackle.

'One small step for man, one giant leap for mankind'.

Then he does a strange almost balletic walk, bouncing on the moon's grey surface before planting a Stars and Stripes flag in the ground.

Well, isn't anything possible now, I think? How long till we get to Mars and meet the Martians: another five years?

It's described as a 'space race' which, at least for today, the Americans seem to have won. It seems to matter a lot that while the Russians had been the first into space, the Americans had made this conquest first today: the Stars and Stripes rather than the Hammer and Sickle, planted by a capitalist not a communist on another territory. I think they call it a Cold War.

My school holidays have just begun, but it is going to be a holiday like no other. I have made a work plan, not set by my school as such, but one of my own devising.

I am going to be sitting the Oxford and Cambridge University entrance exams this December and I can't waste a single day till then. I found it difficult to choose between English and History as my chosen subject but I have plumped in the end for the latter.

I asked my teacher what I should do to prepare. She just said read, read, read. She had some suggestions, but no reading list – in reality she left it to me.

I needed to have a broader knowledge than the core curriculum of Tudors and Stuarts. So I went to the libraries at school and in town and just borrowed and read anything historical that I could find on the shelves.

Anything, that is, up to about the mid-Victorian years, when the mainly British history I needed to know about seemed to end. Anything more recent than a hundred years ago didn't really count as history.

I set myself to read one book every day. Sometimes I make full notes, sometimes I simply try to commit the key points to memory. I am very good at memorising things – especially dates.

As well as a work plan, I am going to allow myself set time off too. On a sunny day, I will go for a walk in Knighton park, or to the lido which is about a twenty-minute walk away

I can also read outside in our back garden in my orange shorts and halter top. Mum's worried about this as it exposes my bare midriff to the sun, and she's worried I'll get burned. The sun never shone on the yard of our old house next to the club so the risk of sunstroke was negligible there.

She's also worried about what I'm eating, or rather what I am not eating. Although I have lost loads of weight since I was thirteen, I am never satisfied. As well as my work plan, I have a diet plan too.

It's also one of my own devising. Lots of protein – brain food as Mum calls it, salads, fruit, some cheese, but no sweets and just two slices of brown bread a day. If I go to bed, feeling hungry, I think the diet must be working.

What my study plan does not allow for is time off in the evening. Mum and Dad would still take a dim view of my going out into Leicester with girlfriends after dark, and I have stopped asking now. I don't want to get distracted.

I would have no time for boyfriends that's for sure – not that I get any opportunities to meet boys except at the bus stop, the tennis club adventure being history.

I saw one of the tennis club boys in the Town Square one day recently. He was in a group of lads from his school. He ignored me – and I ignored him. We're both sixth formers now, and feel embarrassed about our fifteen-year-old selves.

Now that it is the school holidays, there's zero risk of such unplanned encounters. It must have been a relief for Mum and Dad, as not long ago at school the perils of going out on the town had been revealed. Not one but two of my classmates had disappeared suddenly from the classroom.

None of the teachers told us where they had gone, but word spread unofficially. I was getting changed for games, when I heard about it from a classmate, a girl who prided herself on knowing everything that was going on.

It seemed that one of our class, a tall, blonde sixteen-year-old, who Mum would describe as an 'early developer', had been going out to clubs in Leicester, where they played American soul music. It was rumoured that she had a boyfriend who was West Indian. What was certain was that she was pregnant and that's why she had left school.

Then only a few weeks later, another girl, the school caretaker's daughter, was also expelled for the same reason. I never heard anything about who her boyfriend was. Even though she lived in a house by the school gate we never saw sight nor sound of her again. I am pretty sure they both had their babies: having an abortion, even if it was now possible to have one legally, would have been even more shameful for girls like us. Adoption was the preferred course.

Our Headteacher, Miss Myra Pedley, was a strong disciplinarian and very keen on keeping up what she saw as high standards of behaviour. I don't suppose she would have had any hesitation in removing these two girls from the school without ceremony nor right of appeal, bringing their education to an abrupt full stop.

I can imagine she'd told them they'd 'ruined' their lives before they had turned seventeen. That's how Mum would have described it too – although with sorrow rather than condemnation.

None of us knew whether Miss Pedley showed anything but anger behind the headmistress's door but she had a fearsome reputation. I was one of the lucky ones fortunate never to be called in to her study for a talking to about some transgression of school rules.

Miss Pedley must have found the Sixties very trying. She would call out girls for such offences as: removing their school hats, removing their hair bands and literally letting their hair down, hitching up their knee-length skirts dangerously close to thigh length to improvise mini-skirts. All of these she summarised as girls 'flaunting their wares'.

She also kept us at arms' length from the boys' school down the road. We learned that our English teacher, one of the few men who taught in the school, had been vetoed from organising a drama production with his counterpart at Wyggeston Boys'.

His argument that it might broaden our potential repertoire and avoid girls having to play all the male roles foundered on the rock of Myra Pedley's opposition. We were told that it was because of her feminist concern that the boys would take control of the production. Some of us thought it was more about what she suspected her girls might be lured into in the heady atmosphere of close contact on the stage.

Mum and Dad were stalwart supports of Miss Pedley.

Last month, Dad got another new job. I think he'd enjoyed life on the buses, so I wasn't sure at first why he'd applied for an office job instead. Maybe for him it was to do with the pension. Dad was well into his fifties now and becoming a clerk in the City Council Housing Department came with membership of a local authority pension scheme. He could accrue ten years' worth of contributions by the time he was due to retire at the age of sixty-five.

You might think Mum would be pleased that Dad's new job would mean she would see more of him in the evening, especially when I go to university next year. I didn't think that was the reason though. I believe she thought an office job, what they call a white collar one, was more respectable than being on the buses.

She was, I know, keenly aware that 'father's occupation' had to go down on the University application form. Our address, of course, was already much more respectable these days.

There was one more change, designed, I felt, at least in part, to help me secure a place at university. Since we'd moved here, Dad had changed the order from the newsagent. Instead of the Mirror and the People, the boy now delivered the Telegraph and the Express on Sunday.

In part, I say, because although Mum worried I might be asked about the family's reading tastes as well as current affairs at my university interview, Dad voted Conservative now. He liked Mr Heath the new Tory leader and was going to vote for him when the election came. Dad liked the fact that he was not from the aristocratic classes like his predecessors but was a grammar school boy from a modest background.

Dad also persisted in his view that the Labour Prime Minister Wilson, half his cabinet and many trade union leaders were all closet communists and were 'ruining' the country. I decide not to argue with him.

I didn't agree with most of what Dad has to say these days. I just get on with my work.

Chapter Eleven

Langley, 2017

10 am Friday morning, one week on from my meeting at the OPG and another day of revelation ahead.

I am back at the same bus stop where I alighted yesterday. Now I have my bearings it seems a much less desolate place than it did before. There are more people about and I am travelling much lighter.

The little community bus turns up on time and I am soon away from the city and onto British Columbia Highway 10, known locally as Glover Road and to Cousin Jessie as the Trunk Road. Within a couple of miles or so, I am passing through Milner.

I crane my neck around but there is not much to see. A barn-like place called Milner Feed and Pet Supply is one of the few buildings I spot.

Very soon Milner is behind us and we are going under the Trans-Canada Highway and past a golf course. It's not long till we arrive at the tourist town of Fort Langley, a place clustered round the National Heritage site which gives it its name.

I get off the bus on a street lined with cafes and shops and close by the Centennial Museum where I have an appointment with Kobi Christian, the Arts and Heritage Curator. I am early and so I have time for a coffee.

Arrested by a life-size puppet of Elvis in the window, I walk into a café which is dedicated to the 50s and to Presley. It's not quite my period, nor Cousin Jessie's although we both lived through the reign of this particular king. There are few customers this morning and the jukebox is silent, so I can sit in peace and get my thoughts together.

I don't really know what to expect Ms Christian will have for me. All I can really think of is that grave I will stand in front of after this first appointment of the day.

Reinforced by caffeine, I am soon standing in front of the museum and then waiting in the small reception area for Ms Christian. I can immediately sense that this meeting will be rather different from the one last week in the city offices of the OPG.

Ms Christian, or Kobi as she's happy to be called, is younger than I imagined from my e mail correspondence. She is in her late thirties, maybe forty and looks quite unlike one's cliched expectation of someone called a Heritage Curator.

She greets me warmly and takes me into her small windowless office. The lack of windows is the only thing this meeting room has in common with the OPG's last Friday. Kobi sits down at a large white table and invites me to sit opposite her.

She has a few documents and a couple of books already laid out in front of her and I take the photographs I have brought with me out of my handbag. It feels like something to trade with her, if you like – just as the men of the Hudson Bay trading company had done with the people of the First Nations, resident on this stretch of the Fraser Valley, when they opened the fort for business not far short of a couple of hundred years ago.

Kobi hands me copies of two documents which she has extracted from the archive. First comes a chart showing the one hundred-acre plots into which the Hudson Bay trading company had split their vast farm in the last years of the nineteenth century. No doubt this was virgin forest before British men, under armed protection, cleared the trees and, later, other British men with rulers carved out these neat rectangles to sell them off to immigrant farmers.

Handwritten on the chart were the names of the first purchasers. Kobi points to George Underwood's name and the date of sale, 1889. Next to it, I see an equally familiar name, that of McDonald. An Alexander McDonald was George's neighbour.

I had seen his name as well as other McDonalds living on Langley Prairie in the old directories I'd accessed before my visit. I'd thought at first that this McDonald might have been the connection bringing Jessie here but I had dismissed this along with the theory of Jessie's marriage to a McDonald some time ago. Alexander had died and his farm had been sold on years before Jessie arrived here.

I see that next to the McDonald plot is one bought by a Worrell. I have seen that name before too: on Jessie and George's wedding certificate.

Another farming family, called Mufford, bought several plots and then there is one in the name of the minister, the Reverend Dunn. Kobi sees me poring with close interest over the chart and offers to send me a copy digitally later. I am grateful not least because I won't need to use my iPad to record everything, as I had to this time last week.

The second document Kobi offers me is quite a curiosity – how has this found its way into the archive? It is a photocopy of a receipt, dated October 1923, from a firm of memorial stone masons for the headstone of George Underwood and, curiously, is addressed to Mr G Underwood Esq even though it was issued more than two years after his death.

Maybe it was intended for the other George, his nephew, George Underwood Walker who it seemed took on the farm after Jessie left. I make a note to check him out again when I get the chance. I am not surprised that it wasn't Jessie who ordered the headstone when I see the cost, $100, a sum four times the amount she brought with her to Canada.

Next Kobi shows me some photographs of Milner as it was at the time Jessie arrived here. There's a picture of the Methodist Church, which was the only church there in 1920 (the Presbyterian Reverend Dunn having moved on by that time). I know that Jessie and George were married at home by the Methodist minister but I expect George's funeral service the following year would have taken place here.

Next is a photograph of the community school, which according to Mrs Kerr, Willie attended for '*some years.*' I ask Kobi if she could check whether a Miss Olson was a teacher there. I tell her that back home I have a small Christmas card from an E. Olson sent to Master Willie Underwood in 1924 and clearly treasured – either by him or by Jessie throughout their lives.

Kobi doesn't have to look it up in a book – she knows already that Miss Olson was a much-loved schoolteacher who long-standing residents of the area remembered well. Another piece of the jigsaw falls into place as Kobi points out this teacher's name in a local record.

Kobi says she has lived in the Langley area all her life and that she runs the community history group. I tell her that I feel fortunate to have met just the right person to help me with my quest, although I describe it to her as a straightforward genealogical one.

I don't tell her about the windfall inheritance, nor my discoveries at the OPG. Something is holding me back: I think it is my suspicion that if anyone does remember Cousin Jessie, they might not have fond memories of her – that they might subscribe to the hostile narrative which Mrs Kerr's and Mrs Bell's words suggested.

I am also giving little away, as I remember a gentle warning from Mrs Jenkins, my original OPG contact, when I broached the idea of using some of my windfall on a trip to Canada. She hinted, but would give no details, that there were some people who didn't take too kindly to William Underwood's inheritance going to Jessie's distant family in England.

There's certainly no suggestion of any of this from Kobi but she does say one thing that strikes me. She thinks – quite understandably given all the road name changes over the years – that I might be confused which of the two Langley properties where Jessie lived was which. She remarks that the farm would have been too much for Jessie to cope with after George died.

It reminds me of what people who didn't know me that well said when I sold my house in the country. Of course, they'd say, you want to leave – it's too much for you now. I would nod in agreement, as it was easier not to tell them that it was much more complicated than that.

Yes, on the face of it, it wasn't surprising that a slightly-built housekeeper with a small child would not stay long in a big house with a hundred acres of land. Still, it wasn't just that letter of Mrs Bell's which suggested that, however unrealistic it might seem, Jessie might have wanted to stay put.

I've seen a Canadian census from 1921, a survey taken only a few months after George died. Jessie now head of the household declares the property on the Trunk Road as her own farm. It looks as if whoever recorded the entry had first handwritten '*farmer*' as Jessie's occupation, then written over it with a word that looks like '*manager*.' A woman in the 1920s might be described as a manager but not a farmer it seems.

Kobi leaves her most exciting news to last. She says she is hopeful that she can put me in touch with one of the veterans in her history group, perhaps as soon as later this morning. Could this be someone who knew Cousin Jessie herself? A ripple of anticipation and just a little apprehension passes through me.

Now it's my turn. I spread the photographs I have brought with me out on the table.

I suggest to Kobi that perhaps the ones I could not identify might be familiar to someone in her history group. Maybe someone would recognise the studio photograph of a pretty girl, ten years or so of age, in a white *broderie anglaise* dress in an old-fashioned style?

Or perhaps the informal shot of a group of middle-aged women in clothes of the 1920s era standing by a farm door was familiar?

Or what about the lone woman, again in 1920s dress, by a farmhouse of a similar style to George's, with the signature 'Janet' on the back?

Perhaps someone might recognise their own mother or father as a child in the school photo I've also brought along. This is the one of William, in a belted jacket, his place in the line-up marked with a cross. He is one of thirty children, boys and girls, posing with a young teacher standing proudly alongside them. I feel confident now that this must be Miss Olson. This picture is the one inscribed on the back, in pencil, Mrs J Underwood with that long, complicated address '*on the road to Cloverdayl*'.

Kobi asks me if she can photocopy all of the photographs. Of course, I tell her. I am more than happy for her to do that.

She goes off to an adjacent room where the scanner is housed, leaving me to peruse further the books and documents she has found for me.

Then the lights go out.

I wait for a few minutes until Kobi returns with the news that the whole area around Fort Langley has lost power. It will take at least an hour she says for the electricity to be restored.

She has a proposition: would I like to go out with her for a drive around the neighbourhood? I realise she is offering to be my very own tour guide.

This is much more than I was expecting or had any reason to hope for. My luck is in again. In the space of the next hour or so Kobi will take me on a guided tour of the landmarks of Jessie and William's lives.

We drive out of the town, back down the Glover Road,

returning on the route I had come by bus. Within a few minutes, we reach what remains of the Milner Jessie knew.

Kobi confirms what I had feared: that the original farmhouses, the stores and even the station had long gone. Yes, the area was still fertile farmland, and there were a few old buildings that survived but where are the people? It is mid-morning on a weekday but still there is no-one about at all.

We turn off the main highway opposite the Milner Feed and Pet Supply store, the timber-clad place I had spotted from the bus and which was at least reminiscent of the original farming settlement. Just metres away from the turn-off, we come to the first stop.

This is Milner Chapel which Kobi tells me had been the Methodist Church which Jessie and George would have known. I read the signboard which shows that it is no longer an active church, but is preserved as a heritage site by the community association. The church, I read, was founded in 1885 after a fundraising drive by local farmers – so perhaps George had contributed. Now the pretty white-painted clapboard building with its needle-shaped spire has lost its congregation and is locked to passing visitors like myself.

I take a couple of photographs and jump back up into Kobi's car. A short distance further on, we turn right into a road named Worrell Crescent (it seemed that several of the roads around here had been named after the first farmers).

We park up again and find ourselves in the grounds of a place called the Hebron Education Centre. This, Kobi tells me, was the site of the Milner School. There's no sign of any children now; there's a playground but it is silent.

I can only imagine the sounds of childish games and fights, with Miss Olson refereeing her charges. Can I discern the ghost of that boy in the belted jacket?

One more photo and I am back in the car again. We double back onto the Glover Road driving south once more in the Langley direction. After barely a minute, Kobi pulls up just off the main road into a lay-by alongside an open field. We are in sight of a big sweeping junction where the highway meets a road which my map tells me is called Mufford Crescent. Ah, the Muffords! – another of the local farming dynasties whose names I have seen countless times in the directories as well as on the old chart this morning.

Kobi invites me to get out and I survey the peaceful scene. She quietly but firmly declares that somewhere just about here she reckons lay George Underwood's one hundred acres and the farmhouse where he lived.

As I step down onto the track by the field, I know my journey to Canada has been for moments like this. I am walking onto what remains of Jessie's first home on the prairie. Amidst the gently rustling grass, isn't there another ghost here, that of the Englishwoman dressed in her old-fashioned blouse and skirt peering uneasily at me?

Running parallel to the road and just a few metres ahead I see a single-track railway line, with telegraph poles standing sentinel along its length. This surely was the line along which Jessie had first arrived from Vancouver.

Crossing the line and running straight ahead towards some more modern farm buildings, a tarmacked track is laid out before me. On the horizon, there is a line of fir trees, thin and gaunt, like those in the old photographs.

I have no binoculars, but using my camera, I zoom in on what looks like a farmhouse but it is of a much more recent vintage than George Underwood's and is obscured by those trees. My gaze returns to the path around me. As well as power lines, wild flowers and shrubbery also border the track.

The fields are either lying fallow or maybe serve as pasture for cows, although I can see none today. The empty land stretches to both left and right, while closest to me and the railway track, a line of tall grasses sways in the warm late summer breeze.

I hear them whispering their memories to me.

Milner, Langley, 1920

On a hot July afternoon, five people emerge onto the veranda overlooking the ripening corn, gently nodding bearded heads in the barely-perceptible breeze. First comes a slim woman, dressed plainly in a white cotton blouse and a long dark skirt, then a bowed old man with a shock of white hair, wearing his Sunday best suit.

They are not as they appear: an elderly father with a dutiful daughter, perhaps. No, they are newly-weds.

They have just exchanged the vows recited to them by the Methodist minister who appears next through the door. He, like the groom is wearing a suit and is carrying a prayer book.

Then come the witnesses: a young couple. Alice Worrell has come to this strange wedding straight from her farmhouse kitchen next door and her brother George from the fields.

The older George had struggled to sign his signature on the register – he has some stiffness in his hands these days and doesn't have much regular practice nor need of handwriting. Jessie had a firmer hand as she wrote her name, McDonald and her status, widow.

She had to pause though over the next lines in the marriage document requiring father's name and mother's maiden name to be inscribed. What to say?

The pen hangs over the page for less time than it takes for the minister to notice. James Heading is written in the first line, and Hattie Rooke in the second. Why pluck the name 'James' out of the sultry air?

Well, why not? Who was ever going to check? Just as no-one needed to know who'd fathered Willie.

Oh yes, where was the boy? He must have slipped away into the field to play until called in for the promised special tea.

No-one was more surprised than Alice and George to be asked to come around to witness the marriage. Old George Underwood who they had known all their lives was not the marrying kind they'd thought. Mrs McDonald, who they'd met only a year ago when she'd arrived out of the blue to become his housekeeper, was much closer in age to them than the old farmer and had been the one who'd asked them to do this special favour for George and her. A matter of fact request, it seemed; asked, not pleaded for, as if Jessie was needing something of little more emotional import than a mug of sugar till she could get to the store.

Alice didn't think it was a love match – well, Mrs McDonald was hardly a giddy young girl, was she? Jessie told her simply that the couple got along fine and – well, it was the decent thing.

Of course. Alice and her brother weren't ones to pry further – they were just happy to help. As for the Minister, if he had a view on the union he'd sealed today before God, he did not disclose it.

The unlikely bride now calls out to the boy to come in for tea. Jessie has prepared some egg sandwiches and a sponge cake with icing. Alice has brought along some scones filled with thick cream and home-made strawberry jam.

The Minister says he will take a cup of tea, thank you, but can't stay long. Alice and George will leave soon too – there's work to do on the farm.

No fuss, no frills, no rings –and no photographs.

Langley, 2017

The sound of a car speeding by behind me cuts rudely through my imaginings and brings me back to the here and now. I turn around towards the highway and see on the other side, a house old enough to have been built by one of George's neighbours.

Kobi notices the direction of my gaze and tells me that she believes this building – one of the very last of the original homes – is scheduled for demolition soon. I can see the community association has quite a struggle on its hands to keep the Milner heritage alive in anything but their own fading memories. I tell Kobi I am glad I haven't waited any longer to make this journey.

While I have been engrossed, she has been sitting in the car making calls but, clearly, she has got no reply from whoever she is trying to raise for me to talk to.

Never mind. It's time for me to get back into the car and we drive on.

The Milner ghosts left behind, we go back the two or three miles to what is now called Langley Centre, close to the bus stop where my day had started. We turn down 204th Street and into the car park of what looks like a 1970s-era office building. The Canadian flag flutters from a pole outside the entrance and over the lobby is a sign, Langley Lodge.

I know now where we are. This is the nursing home where William Underwood died twenty-three years before.

I get out and take a couple of photographs but do not go in. I had not had any response when I had sent an email from England some weeks ago inquiring whether there were any long-standing members of staff who might remember William. I knew it was a long-shot and it seems there weren't.

There was no need to keep Kobi waiting here. The tour resumes.

We go back a few blocks north, and I find myself again on 56th Avenue. Kobi has certainly done her homework, as she drives straight to our next destination.

She parks up in front of an undistinguished two-storied commercial building which does not bear a number but surely it must be No. 19779. Can this be Jessie's second home in Langley?

Can this, rather than the Milner field, be the place where that photograph of Jessie and William standing in front of their shack, half-hidden by grass was taken?

Unlike the one of George's substantial farmhouse which he'd sent to his sister, I can't imagine that Jessie ever posted a picture of her humble place to anyone back home – not to Kate Muncey, nor to Daisy Fromant, because surely if there had been any correspondence with them, their letters would have been kept with Jessie's other mementoes.

That photograph of Cousin Jessie with her child, I have left at home, too precious for me to risk losing it on this journey. Still, I can see it in my mind's eye now and for sure, I struggle to match it with what I see before me.

I get out of the car to take in the mundane scene. The signs indicate that this is where a masonry firm and a small manufacturing company do business. A grey brick-built building with a grey-painted corrugated iron roof, this is the sort of place that does not draw attention to itself. Evergreen shrubbery shields the site from the road and a bus stop.

I look behind me and across the street is a different aspect with a smart-looking apartment building running the length of the block. I now see the street signs which show we are at the junction of 56th and 198th Street.

Yes, we are in the right place: No. 19799, the place Jessie described as being on the '*road to Cloverdayl*' on the back of that school photo I have left in the photocopying room in Fort Langley – the '*small home in Langley City.*'

I walk around the back. A large and almost empty tarmacked yard has long replaced the garden. There would have been plenty of room here for Cousin Jessie and William to grow fruit and vegetables and keep a few chickens. Time enough too, as this was the place Jessie and William occupied for all of seventy years.

The only vegetation I see now are a few weeds and some yellowing grass which has sprung up next to the metal fence. I look over the back and see a builder's yard with some scaffolding and pallets. Further beyond that lies the industrial estate of Production Way.

So this is it – the source of my inheritance: this featureless and non-descript two acres. I struggle to conjure up any ghosts here.

I wish I had brought with me the photographs I have in my box file, taken here when William was an old man. This showed a small brick-built dwelling set back a little way from the highway and with a large industrial building next to it. There is a close-up of him standing by the door.

I have no idea when the shack was pulled down and replaced by the sturdier if still modest bungalow where William was captured for prosperity. By the 1990s his home would have stood out like a sore thumb in an increasingly industrial scene.

I have no photos of Jessie in that brick-built home, nor of her taken anywhere else in her fifty years in Langley township. There's nothing more recent than that first haunting photograph taken around 1922. How could she have lived so long without a single picture?

Now I see that everything Jessie and William had called home had been demolished by the company which bought the property from the Office of the Public Guardian, who'd sold it to fund William's nursing care. There was of course more than enough remaining from the sale to provide a handsome bequest to ten distant beneficiaries.

I can – at last – understand why this became prime real estate. Once only the most modest of properties with land enough for a smallholding on the edge of a growing township, by the 1990s it was well-placed for commercial development and within easy reach of the Trans-Canada Highway. It was well-situated too for other key routes and close to the American border, so at a hub linking Vancouver's trade to the rest of the Canadian Federation as well as to the United States.

Location, location, location, as the Canadian realtors might say. Asset appreciation, as the money men call it. Home Sweet Home, as Jessie and William knew it, pulled down in no time at all with a wrecking ball.

It was a property that offered them not wealth but nearly fifty more years of hard work, few material comforts and no easy retirement for Jessie nor her son either. I – and my equally comfortable cousins – were the lucky ones: fortunate, but not deserving – the unlikely beneficiaries of one Canadian immigrant's American dream.

I stand for a few minutes in this soulless place and quietly thank Cousin Jessie for her life's work. I have no appetite to knock at the office door.

I've seen enough.

Above: George Underwood, Langley, British Columbia (c1910)
Below: Jessie with William, Langley, B.C (c1922)

Margaret Bell, George's sister, Dumfries, Scotland (c1910)

Above: Milner School, Langley, with William Underwood
back row, far left (c1925)
Below: The house on 56th Avenue, Langley B.C (post-1970,
date unknown)

Above: William Underwood, Langley B.C (post-1970, date unknown)

Below: The author, Fort Langley Cemetery (September 2017)

Chapter Twelve

Fort Langley, 2017

I t's too late to buy flowers.

I am quietly reprimanding myself for my thoughtlessness as Kobi slows down and turns off the road again. This is the highlight – if I can call it that – not just of today's trip but of this past week in Canada.

No, more than that, it is where my steps have been leading for the past two years. We have arrived at Fort Langley cemetery.

The place where the ghosts of Milner found eternal rest was an unshowy place, easily missed if I had not had my own tour guide. It was of course a quiet spot, but seemed, given its history and its location close to the fort, pretty understated.

There's a modest sign at the entrance, indicating that Fort Langley is one of the oldest cemeteries in British Columbia, opened in 1881, the year the British census had recorded a particular four-year-old illegitimate child in Cambridge, living a stone's throw from another Victorian cemetery.

I reckon, for Cousin Jessie, it would have been a good hour's walk to the north of Milner on the Glover Road and another hour from her second home. It would not have been an easy place for her to visit to mourn her husband of eight months, even if she had had the time and energy to do so.

It was a rather smaller place than I had imagined, covering

maybe ten acres; a flat and featureless rectangular field with its monuments and headstones set well apart from each other. It's quite unlike the sprawling, overcrowded and overgrown Victorian cemeteries I am familiar with at home, Mill Road in Cambridge among them.

More of those gaunt fir trees patrol the cemetery perimeter, as if the site has only been recently reclaimed from the forest. There are few visitors this morning.

Kobi parks up close to the spot where the cemetery staff, who knew I was visiting that day, had put markers on the road to help us find the grave. She holds back, I realise respecting that I might wish for a few minutes on my own.

For sure, I am apprehensive as I approach a granite headstone but as I reach it, I realise it is not Jessie's but that of her farmer husband. It's the monument I now know was purchased for $100 two years after he died.

It stands as solid and seemingly eternal as the one I had found of his sister Margaret in an equally quiet Scottish graveyard just a month before. The inscription is clearly legible: George Underwood, born February 23 1845, died March 29 1921.

A few metres to the left I find a much newer stone plaque set into the neatly mown grass. This reads even more simply: William Underwood 1915–1994.

'Jessie's in the middle.'

Kobi has quietly left the car and stands now within earshot. She steps back again, as I step forward.

I move to stand on the grass between the headstone and the plaque, where Cousin Jessie's headstone should have been and where her mortal remains lie.

Unmarked.

Unrecognised as George's widow.

Unmourned, it seems… until now.

For some reason, I could not yet fathom, the man who she claimed as her son had not spent any of the savings his mother had left him on any sort of memorial for her. A son, who a quarter of a century after his mother's death, with no family to mourn him was honoured by this plaque, erected by a public body into whose care he had been taken. The Canadian state had given William dignity in his modest death.

Jessie had no such recognition or honour. Here she lies, somehow illegitimate to the end, erased from memory, written off the slate of humanity, until this day.

Kobi offers to take a photograph of me. I am smiling in that photo but inside I am weeping for Cousin Jessie, more in anger than in sorrow.

I realise there would have been nowhere to put any flowers, except to strew them on the grass. In this moment, I resolve that one day I will come back to honour her properly, to have a headstone carved: Jessie Ashbowl Underwood, formerly Heading, born Cambridge, England, January 25 1877, died Langley City, June 17 1970.

Maybe underneath this, I'd have a suitable text from her birthday book inscribed. No, better surely, to add just two simple words: 'Not forgotten'.

After all, she wasn't such a distant cousin, but someone who had been just a telephone call away. Someone who might have watched on a little black and white television in Langley, B.C. the same astonishing events that I had on mine in Leicester.

She might have been stunned as I was by the awful events of November 1963 when President Kennedy was shot, to be followed in a ghastly procession of American assassinations and civil turmoil, by Martin Luther King's and then by the second Kennedy.

She might have watched on the local news the mayhem as the mop-headed boys from Liverpool took Vancouver by storm just two months before I saw them at the De Montfort Hall.

Finally, in the last year of her life, she could have been amazed as I was by that first moon landing celebrating that famous giant leap for mankind. What did Jessie make of that extra-terrestrial expedition, I wonder, coming half a lifetime as it had after her own transatlantic and cross-continental journey? A trip which for a young woman who had never travelled before, and alone, took the same sort of courage and faith, for which those astronauts were hailed.

As I stand here quietly, almost certainly the first person to come here to mourn this woman, I think how it might have been different. That will I saw for the first time in Vancouver last week comes to my mind-the proof I have that her natural mother had not forgotten her only child. A Victorian woman who seems to have been denied any choice but to abandon her baby girl into the care of a stranger, settled for a life of spinsterhood with her elderly father, with her sister's legitimate boy child to nurse instead.

Would Jessie have gone to Canada if she'd known her real mother's love and could have lived a quiet respectable country life as a farmer's daughter and perhaps later a Bedfordshire farmer's wife?

Yes, would she have risked all if she'd known that she would live all of fifty-eight years in a distant country, where she had to work hard all her life, unsupported, where she 'made few friends' and was at the end laid to rest in an unnamed plot.

Yes, she was an ordinary woman, her life, some would say, was without distinction and made no mark on the society in which she lived – but it was not without bravery and dignity, that's for sure. She was somebody's daughter and somebody's 'mother', as well as my cousin Jessie. Was there so little reward for volunteering to be a 'daughter of the Empire'?

Here she lies six feet beneath this turf, where I now stand, the lucky one, better off by twenty thousand pounds, thanks to my cousin's hard work, the long bachelorhood of her son, the roulette wheel of the property market and the rules of intestacy. At least, I comfort myself, she lies in a good place – amongst those who her generation would have called the pioneers.

She was laid to rest here in this foreign field without much ceremony, no doubt, far away from where the winds of change were blowing away at last those lethal cobwebs that were the Victorian prejudices which had ensnared her life. In the Midlands city where I lived, that Sixties whirlwind bringing a revolution in social mores especially for women, hadn't yet quite swept those cobwebs away.

Six months before Cousin Jessie died, a visit to the same English university town where she was born into a life of genteel servitude is the first step towards my own liberation.

Leicester, 1969.

After my long summer of rigorous preparation and equally rigorous diet and exercise regime then a final period of intensive study at school, I am about to be tested. One other girl and I have just sat the series of special papers set by Oxford and Cambridge Universities for entry next year.

I had to choose two colleges to put down as my first choices, one at Oxford and one at Cambridge. There are only five colleges, all women's of course, to select from in Oxford and a mere three in Cambridge. For all I know about them, I might as well write the names on a strip of paper, put them in a tub and take pot luck.

In the end, I do find a couple of reasons to choose Lady Margaret Hall in Oxford: one, it has a river running through the garden, which I like the sound of and two, more importantly, there was another girl at my school two years above me, who teachers tell me won a place there.

I really can't remember why I chose Girton at Cambridge and why I opted for Cambridge above Oxford as my top choice. There have been no open days and I had never visited either city, so I had no idea what to expect. Could it have been because Joan Bakewell who I liked from the telly went there?

When I am offered interviews at both places, I am shocked and it causes quite a flurry, not just of excitement in Mum and Dad. They think I need to buy a suit for the interview. We are not expected to go in school uniform and I have a limited wardrobe given my few social outings.

The interviews are in a just a few days so there is no time to lose. Mum and I go shopping in the sort of shops we never usually visit. Fenwick and Marshall and Snelgrove's ladies' departments are not really the sort of places a teenager would want to go.

Mum thinks I will need a new coat too as it's December. Rather than a suit, we end up buying a matching dress and coat in a boucle wool, black, with green piping, the dress a safe one inch above knee-length. Very smart and it fits my now petite frame well, but, in truth, it's the sort of outfit a forty-year-old might wear to a job interview or a winter wedding.

Well, what did I know? What pleases me most is that I am now a size 10.

We are expected to stay overnight at the colleges, but there is no money for a second outfit, so this will have to do for the four days in all that I will be away attending the interviews in the coming week.

On day one, Dad drives me from Leicester to Cambridge. It seems to take ages, but as my interview is not till the following morning, I am not too worried. We don't see anything of Cambridge itself though. Girton College is on the outskirts of town on the side we first arrive at via the A604 from Huntingdon.

It's only now I realise that Girton is about three miles from the centre of town, and that it will be a good hour's walk to lectures or maybe a fifteen-minute cycle ride if I get the hang of riding one and if it doesn't rain too much.

Dad leaves me at the gate. He is going to go straight home and come back tomorrow afternoon.

I see a red brick Gothic pile looming in front of me. What does it remind me of? A girls' boarding school perhaps. I have never seen one in real life but I've read Malory Towers.

No, that's it, it reminds me of the Towers, where my mum had been treated after her breakdown the best part of six years ago. It did not look very welcoming.

I go inside and am introduced to a first-year student, who smiles and radiates blithe assurance. Rather than a mini skirt she is wearing a long flowing floor-length one as if she is something out of a Gothic novel.

She takes me down a very long, straight wood-panelled corridor to the room where I am going to spend the night. This too brings to mind a Victorian melodrama.

It all feels very disorienting and I don't feel at all comfortable trying to sleep in some other girl's room for one night, let alone the prospect of spending three years here. I am very rapidly going off my top choice college.

Despite the best endeavours of the friendly tutors who interview me the next morning and the student assigned to make me feel at home, I cannot dispel my initial horror of the place.

When Dad picks me up, and he asks me how it went, I say that I think it went alright and that I liked the college. How can I possibly disappoint him?

There is no time to spend seeing the sights in the centre of the city. We set off straightway for home.

I tell Dad I expect to hear within a week or so whether I have been offered a place. I am now a lot more nervous than I let on – not of failing to be offered a place but of being successful.

The next morning, I am off again, this time to Oxford and by the train. Summer holiday steam trains aside, this is the first time I have travelled this way and, at the age of seventeen and a half, the first time I have gone anywhere on my own.

So the trip to Oxford takes on a rather more exciting dimension long before I get to my destination. After changing trains at Birmingham, I get into conversation with a young woman called Mary who is also on her way to Oxford and to the same college as me.

She goes to boarding school somewhere in the Home Counties and she wants to study English. She speaks impeccably and I realise my elocuted vowels don't quite match her genuine accent.

She is also effortlessly well-dressed. I feel for the first time that my coat and dress ensemble isn't quite right. She is wearing a neat little jumper, with a scarf tied just so around her neck, along with a kilt-type of skirt, which is about two inches shorter than mine. How I think those two inches improve the look!

We arrive at the college together and wish each other good luck. I can't remember for the life of me anything I am asked at the interview. What impressed me was seeing women with more bookshelves in their rooms than I have ever seen before. Books to the ceiling indeed! Whether they inquired about my newspaper reading habits or what my father did for a living escapes my memory.

All I recall was the final meeting I had with an elderly woman with a twinkle in her eye, who was called Dame Lucy Sutherland. I have never met a dame before, but the college principal seemed friendly enough and her questions weren't too taxing.

Oh, and I remember walking through the garden to see the River Cherwell, with flat-bottomed boats I had never seen before moored by the river's edge. Afterwards, I have time to walk through the Parks from the college into the centre of the city. The streets are lined with old stone buildings, quirky looking shops, pubs and cafes. Although this city is very different from Leicester, I feel I can get used to living in a place like this.

A few days' later, and just a week before Christmas, I get a telegram. That's a first too. It's not like a letter – there's no space for detail – so its message is brief, to the point and thrilling.

LMH is offering me a scholarship, named after someone called Alice. A letter will follow.

Then two days after, a letter arrives from Cambridge, offering me a place there. I know that the offer of a scholarship means Oxford really wants me and the follow-up letter explains that it comes with £100 a year which will go a long way to subsidising my living costs. It isn't hard to decide which to accept.

The school must have rung the local paper with the news because shortly after that, a man from the Mercury comes around to take my photograph for the newspaper. It's a 'local girl makes good' story.

For the first time I can remember, Mum is happy to let someone over our threshold. When the photo is published, though, I am mortified. It is not a flattering portrait.

It isn't just my serious expression; it is the pallor from too much time spent in the library. I look the epitome of – what is the word? – yes, a bluestocking. Those long months of relentless study, all work, and no play, have they made this Jill a dull girl? I fear so.

Is that who I want to be? Is that even who I was as a child? I never wanted to be a professor-I wanted to perform.

My first ambition to be a ballet dancer went out of the window soon enough, with my ballooning weight. Then, I remember, for a while I wanted to be an air stewardess – a job which seemed to promise a life of glamour as well as international travel.

All through my grammar school years, though, I seem to have been on a moving walkway to a very different sort of career. I am the brainy girl, the swot: the one who will be encouraged to learn Latin and Ancient Greek. The girl for whom music lessons, choir and drama are very much light relief from my main mission – to get to Oxbridge and study something serious.

Still, at home, I don't stop dancing in front of the TV. Now rather than the Hollywood musicals I used to watch on those suffocating Sunday afternoons at home in the place next to the Working Men's Club, I'd be aping the dancers on Top of the Pops and Ready Steady Go on Thursday and Friday evenings instead.

So who have I become now? As I look at that dull photograph, of a bespectacled and earnest girl staring stonily at the newspaper man's camera, I recoil. This isn't the real me.

My excitement at going to Oxford is not at all about the opportunity to study more history for three years. It is about the new world that will open up for me.

Before that, I can enjoy Christmas and relax a bit. The New

Year will bring the start of a new decade, as well as my new life. I just somehow have to get through the first nine months of 1970 till I can get on with it.

I am not quite free yet. For one thing, I still have to pass my A levels in June, although as I have an unconditional offer from LMH, I don't have to worry too much about my grades.

Little else changes yet. I still spend most of my time at home. My Saturday nights are spent in front of the television: watching for hours from Dr Who at teatime, through Cilla in the early evening, followed by the Morecambe and Wise Show.

There's still no going out on the town in Leicester. No boyfriends, no partying, but at least it won't be hard to leave behind. I realise that unlike most of my schoolfriends I have no emotional investment in Leicester at all.

My still-cloistered life also has the advantage that I can save up my pocket money for Oxford. For the first time I decide not to buy the latest – and perhaps the last – Beatles LP. Abbey Road doesn't make it to my bedroom shelf.

I have a Dansette record player in my bedroom now, so I spend much more time there rather than in the sitting room with Mum. I am quietly withdrawing from our family life.

I did suggest to Mum and to Dad that I might get a Saturday job to while away the time and earn some of my own money but they were horrified. They didn't want me to become a shop girl, even on a temporary basis. Dad said not to worry, he'd make sure I had enough to live on when I go away.

I suppose I could have just ignored their views but I am still a child and they still exert the same powerful hold on my life. At least while I am under their roof, I will accept their veto, suppressing my desire for independence – and money for a whole new wardrobe – for a while yet.

Fort Langley, 2017

Kobi Christian drives back into the car park at the Centennial Museum. She reminds me that she has not completed the task of copying my photographs, so, assuming the power has returned, she asks me if I can come back in an hour or so.

Before I get out of the car, though, she makes one last attempt on her phone to reach the local woman she is keen for me to speak to. At last someone picks up.

She passes the phone to me. 'This is Ellen Worrell on the line.'

A Worrell, well she hardly needs any introduction to me but I introduce myself and tell her how delighted I am to speak to her.

A strong, if elderly voice responds. 'Yes, I've been doing my own family history research' comes the reply. 'My family lived next door to George Underwood's farm.'

Yes, indeed – hope, even excitement, surges through me. For one minute, I think I might be talking to someone who had actually known Jessie. I did a rapid mental calculation – if Ellen was in her eighties, then it was possible. She was probably born after Jessie left Milner, but still…

I tell Ellen I am interested in George Underwood's wife Jessie – that I am related to her, a distant cousin. That I believe two of the Worrell family witnessed her marriage to George. Yes, Ellen confirms she knows that too. She is George Worrell's daughter-in-law.

That scene I conjured up in the Milner field of a summer marriage on a warm veranda lights up again in my mind. What else might a Worrell know? There is just one urgent question I have for Ellen.

'Do you remember Jessie Underwood?'

Hope ignites briefly, then is immediately extinguished.

No, comes the reply.

Ellen tells me she had lived in the nearby town of Murrayville, where she worked in a bank, for much of her life and had only come to Langley in recent years. She is apologetic that she has no information about Jessie.

It seems she has no stories passed down from the Worrell older generation either. Jessie slips from my grasp again.

I try another tack. 'Did you know her son, William?'

'Oh yes, I knew Bill', she says.

It was the first time I'd heard him referred to this way. No longer the Willie or William of Jessie's birthday book or the official correspondence, but Bill, someone's neighbour, a regular sort of guy – or perhaps not.

'So what was he like?' I say.

There was a pause at the other end of the line. A pause long enough to reinforce a growing intimation I have that William Underwood might have been one of the main reasons that his mother and he 'made few friends'.

'Was he a bit of a …loner?' I venture to encourage a

response from Mrs Worrell.

Something tells me that her hesitation in replying masks uncertainty as to how best to describe someone honestly but without being too damning. She is from that generation who would not speak ill of the dead.

'Yes', Ellen responds now, 'I suppose he was.'

Another pause, then she continues, with this rather puzzling observation. What she always associated with Bill, she tells me, was the great pile of wood outside his place on 56th Avenue.

It wasn't clear whether she meant by this that he ran some sort of timber business from his home or whether it was simply a measure of his eccentricity.

There is little more she has to say. There are no anecdotes nor warm words forthcoming.

Should I have gone further and tried the descriptor 'oddball' rather than 'loner' I wonder? Maybe Mrs Worrell would have thought that too much but perhaps others among her neighbours might not have hesitated to agree with that less polite characterisation.

Sensing that the elderly Mrs Worrell has nothing else to tell me and is tiring of the conversation, I ask whether she knew anyone else still alive who might remember them any better.

'If anyone would around these parts, it would be Hugh, Hugh Davis', she says. Kobi could give me his number.

I will have to check, but I think there was a Davis amongst the original purchasers of the Hudson's Bay trading company farm. If so, then it would be well worth talking to him.

As a rather desperate last shot, I tell Ellen that I am only in the area for a few days and if she remembers any more to please get in touch with Kobi. I thank her for her time and hand the phone back.

As I do, I know I must not lose the opportunity to make one last request. I whisper to Kobi – can she ask Ellen whether we could call in to see her before I leave.

I am not surprised by the answer: no, it would not be possible – she wasn't really up for visitors – she wasn't in the best of health, I'm told.

Sensing my disappointment, Kobi says she hopes that Ellen will be able to look at my photos when she next attends a meeting of the community history group. That won't happen though till sometime after I get back to England. We leave the car and Kobi walks towards her office and tells me she'll see me again in an hour.

I decide to fill the time with a visit to Fort Langley itself which lies a few minutes' walk away. Slipping back into tourist mode again, I walk into the ticket hall. It's free to enter this year, I'm told – a bonus to visitors in this Canadian 150th anniversary year.

I pass through the foyer and am soon outside again. It's cooler now and threatening to rain. For the first time in a while, I put on a jacket.

There are few visitors today so I can take my time going around the site. A few wooden buildings and one brick-built one line the perimeter around the grassy compound, where white canvas tents are erected to mimic the early settlement.

My eyes are drawn to an area with a table and a single chair set by a glassless window hatch. It is framed by shutters and a line of pine fencing made out of whole trunks bound together.

It seems that this is a reconstruction of the place where the nineteenth-century British men of the Hudson's Bay Company did their unequal trade with the First Nations people. It was clearly uneasy business, with the shutters readily shut and barred and the whole enclosure readily defended, by arms if necessary.

I carry on the length of the palisade towards the brick building, where I am invited inside to see the exhibits describing the history of the site. One picture grabs my attention.

The name McDonald stands out in large letters superimposed on the portrait of a smiling whiskered face. I read with consternation the text on the interpretation board:

'Matchmaker, Matchmaker. Thanks to Chief Trader Archibald McDonald, within a year of taking charge of Fort Langley, 17 of his 18 men had Aboriginal wives. He defended these marriages to his superiors – they were good for business.'

Below him, was a picture of his wife, one of these so-called 'Aboriginals' who changed her name to plain Anglo-Saxon Jane. Here she is painted as the epitome of British nineteenth-century womanhood; nothing of her First Nations origins remains. She wears a prim white lace bonnet and beneath her portrait there is a testimonial dated 1835 to her as a 'jewel of rare excellence' and her children (she had thirteen with Archibald) as 'living testimony to her maternal efficiency.'

I had never come across that way of describing fecundity before. If that was the test for success as a woman in these parts then my own Grandmother McDonald with her eleven would have met it, while Jessie with her one illegitimate, possibly sickly child, one I felt was not even the product of her own womb, would have failed again to pass muster.

With the image of that unmarked grave still filling my head, I consider how this man and his prize wife are still honoured here, while Jessie, who came to this area three generations later, is forgotten – and dishonoured.

I walk outside again and see nearby a small compound containing half a dozen kid goats, in a wooden pen, no doubt to entertain child visitors. There are no children today, so I pick up one of the bags of food provided for them to feed the animals. I hold my hand out towards their keening heads for them to nibble the grain from my palm.

'Shall I take a picture for you?' I hear someone say. I hand my fellow-visitor the camera, and put my hand out again to the nuzzling kids.

It puts me in a calmer mood for returning to Kobi's office, to pick up the photos and make my farewells. She insists on calling me a cab and I do not demur, as I am tired and pleased to get back to the B-and-B quickly.

As well as supper, I have much else to chew on this evening.

Chapter Thirteen

Cloverdale, 2017

Saturday morning and I am re-thinking my plans for the weekend.

Until my day in Fort Langley, I had been expecting to spend today tramping around the city by foot trying to find the places which were part of Jessie and William's lives but, of course, Kobi's tour has made that schlep unnecessary.

Lorna, with whom I am getting on famously, has a proposition for me too. She tells me over breakfast that there is an event on today in Cloverdale which might interest me. One of the local heritage groups is running a special trip on the old railway line on one of their restored trains.

She was thinking of going along – would I like to go with her? I say yes, of course, that would be great. It's not till lunchtime though, so I still have a free morning.

Before I leave the B-and-B, I make a couple of calls. I ring Hugh Davis. I reckon it must have been his father who bought one of the Hudson Bay farm plots at the same time as George, although their farms were some way apart. A frail-sounding man picks up. He says it's better if I speak to his sister: maybe he is hard-of-hearing, or maybe just too weak to hold a conversation with a strange woman from England.

He passes on the phone quickly and I relay my questions through his go-between. I am to be disappointed. He doesn't respond to the names of either Jessie or William.

Instead he suggests I speak to a woman called Dawn Ryan. He tells me that her mother was called Ann Underwood Walker and that she was related in some way to George. It seems pointless to extend the conversation, although I tell him, genuinely enough, that it is good to speak to someone from one of the original farming families. His sister gives me Mrs Ryan's number and I end the call.

Feeling rather deflated, as Jessie eludes me again, I wonder whether it's even worth another call. Yet, I realise that I have heard the name of Dawn Ryan somewhere before in the past week. Wasn't it in that letter from the woman who described Jessie and William's arrival in Milner?

I look at Velma Kerr's letter yet again. Yes, Dawn Ryan was indeed one of the three names she had recommended the OPG contact for more information about George Underwood. I hadn't come across her name in my previous research on his family and I think it will be a long shot that she will know anything about Cousin Jessie.

Still I will give her a try. Maybe she will at least know something about the man who Mrs Worrell called Bill.

Dawn is charming and courteous but sadly has little to tell that I don't already know. She's interested in my genealogical pursuit of her family and hopes I can answer questions she has for me rather than being able to answer any of mine. She tells me about an old letter, written on bamboo, that she has inherited from someone called J.J. Underwood. He was a doctor, she tells me, who worked in Hong Kong in the late nineteenth century. She'd love to know how she is related to him.

I tell her I'll look him up when I go to the library. I try to get Mrs Ryan back onto the subject of my interest. Has she heard of Jessie Underwood?

She tells me cheerfully she has a grandson called Jesse as if this co-incidence may be of some import. I say something cheery in response to disguise my disappointment.

What about Bill Underwood? No. Mrs Ryan is even vague on what her relationship to George might be. She does confirm that George Underwood Walker was her grandfather and that he did work the farm but believes it was owned by another family member, an uncle she thinks.

I realise that if the will Jessie apparently put her hopes in had been set aside and George declared intestate, then that might well have been the case. I thought it better not to reveal that there was a dispute involving Jessie after George died.

It sounded to me as if, even if the OPG had followed up the lead Mrs Kerr had given them, Dawn would have had little to tell. Maybe they could have learnt more from her now deceased mother, the woman Hugh Davis called Ann Underwood Walker and who was on Mrs Kerr's contact list as Ann Underwood Mufford.

Mrs Ryan becomes animated when talking about her mother. She tells me how she was born in South Africa (at a time when that country was very much part of the British Empire). How she, along with her family moved to the US, to Washington State, just over the border from British Columbia, and then how she visited Milner as a girl before she came to stay permanently. How she'd fallen in love with a farmer's son, one of the Muffords. How they had courted for more than ten years before their families had allowed them to marry.

Most families have stories they pass from generation to generation and how an Underwood Walker came to marry a Mufford was clearly the romantic one at the top of her mind. George, let alone Jessie and William, did not feature, it seems, in the Underwood folk memory.

I bring the call to a close, telling Mrs. Ryan I'll ring her again if I find out more about J.J. Underwood. I need to go to Cloverdale library again and as it is close to the heritage railway station, I can fit it in before our train ride.

I take the long walk again. It's still overcast, although Lorna has told me there's been rain in the Rockies at last and there's hope the forest fire cloud will lift. We might see the sun again before the weekend's over.

I am back at the crossing on what today is a quieter 56th highway and reach the library in time for their regular Saturday morning family history session. I decide to join the twenty or so local enthusiasts for a talk, aimed at beginners, but which I think will be helpful in understanding more about research in a Canadian context. It's still less than two years since I started my investigations and even though I feel quite an experienced family historian now, I am sure there will be something I can learn here.

It's not long before we are onto the subject of birth, marriage and death statistics or Vitals as they call them here. Our teacher this morning says how their old records are not always complete – Yes, I know about that – and that some of the early immigrants to Canada had things to hide from their past life – Yes, I know about that too.

She gives as example the men who came over the land

border from the US fleeing the law as well as the women who did not want to say too much about who fathered their children. She says that a century ago in some rural communities, there were itinerant preachers, who might only manage to visit each place once a year. Couples often couldn't wait before their unions could be officially signed and sealed, so their marriages might not take place till well after the arrival of their first baby. That wasn't Jessie's situation but I felt that her marriage to George did give her boy some retrospective legitimacy, at least from her perspective, if not from that of her neighbours.

I flick through the handout and am brought up short by a bullet point in bold. 'Whoopsies' it says – a phrase which prior to this, I had only associated with a very old school comedian referring to bodily – accidents shall we say – to raise a cheap laugh.

Then come examples: *non-paternal events*, *adoptions*, *orphans etc.*

In other words, this is a coy reference to illegitimacy and disguised paternity again. I look around me at the mostly elderly audience and wonder if I am the only one who is offended by this.

It's the second decade of the twenty-first century, for goodness sake, I feel like shouting out. I restrain myself and decide to take it on the chin for Cousin Jessie.

Some photocopied documents are passed around. They are samples of Vitals from the early twentieth century.

There's a copy of a Canadian birth certificate from 1901 to peruse. Our lecturer points out there's a lot of useful detail in it: not just date of birth, place of birth, sex and name of child, but also name and maiden surname of mother, residence and rank or profession of father, name of medical attendant and nurse. Finally, there's a space for filling in 'Reason if Father does not report Birth.'

A lot of detail I realise Cousin Jessie might wish to hide from the authorities and reason to cast any document that William might have had into the fire as well. As Canada was very much a British dominion back then, I expect this form of document was modelled on the British one.

It reminds me it wasn't just Jessie who had trouble with such a record.

Leicester, 1970

Mum's in a bit of a state. The council has asked me to supply a birth certificate along with my university grant application. I can't remember having needed to show one before. I've never been abroad, I don't have a passport and so have never had to prove my date of birth before, I suppose. I don't know why it's rattled Mum.

Eventually she digs out a small square certificate on cream-coloured paper with the Crown crest in red at the top, and, handwritten in black ink, my name, my sex, my date of birth, my place of birth – Leicester. Then the name of the registrar, his signature and the date of registration in 1952.

That's all. I can't see what the fuss was about.

I've just turned eighteen. We went out to a posh restaurant

to celebrate my birthday, just Mum, Dad and me. That was a real first. I had fish in a sauce with a French name and a glass of white wine and I felt quite grown-up. I wasn't sure Dad liked the fancy food though and Mum seemed nervous in these surroundings. Hardly surprising, I suppose, given she went out in the evening so rarely, and then not to places like this.

I'm also learning to drive; I had some lessons as a birthday present. Dad says he'll give me extra tuition and practice as well as those I have at the driving school. I was quite nervous on my first proper lesson, trying to navigate narrow terraced streets in Leicester with cars parked along either side. The driving instructor has to use his controls to brake the car more than once, so I think it's going to take me a while to get the hang of it – even with Dad's help. Still, maybe I can pass my test before I go to Oxford.

Shortly after my birthday, comes another rite of passage into the adult world. The Labour Government has just reduced the voting age from twenty-one to eighteen and so I am excited when the General Election is called, knowing I soon will be able to vote for the first time.

It's a warm June day and my exams are over when I walk to the polling station. I take pleasure in putting a cross in pencil on the voting sheet, folding it, and posting it in the black box.

I ask Mum if she remembered the first time she'd voted: it seemed she had to wait until 1945, when she was nearly thirty, as there had been no elections during the war. I had once again been luckier in how things fell for me, just as I have already had nearly five more years of education than she did.

When the election results come in, during the night, it's clear that Mr Wilson is out, and there will be a new Conservative Prime Minister, Edward Heath. Dad's very pleased.

I'm not. I voted Labour.

Cloverdale, 2017

I've arranged to meet Lorna at the old station, which is on the other side of the 56th highway from the library. I hadn't even spotted it on my expedition here a couple of days ago, as it's set back from the road behind a parking lot.

Lorna goes to get the tickets, while I look at the old photographs on the wall. Here is one taken about 1914, showing carriage car number 1225 on Columbia Street, New Westminster at the very time Cousin Jessie was there. For sure, she could have sat on the very car I am looking at now. I can see that the picture was taken very close to the archive building I was in only a few days ago.

The next is captioned 'Glover Road between Milner and Jardine Stations', so close to where Jessie lived with George. This trip on an old train will be more than a holiday outing, surely it will be another encounter with my persistent cousin. Just as I have been flagging, thinking that I am running out of road on my research, it is as if her ghost is haunting me still, calling me not to abandon her just yet.

Lorna gives me a ticket and we go to board the train which

is parked on the platform. Carriage No 1225 stands ready for us – the very same carriage as the one depicted in the old photo in the lobby.

Now I can see its livery is red and white. The paintwork and its brass fittings are positively gleaming, not reflected from the still-absent sunlight but from the elbow grease of the volunteers who have worked to restore it.

Lorna and I climb aboard. Is there a woman in a plain grey floor-length dress waiting patiently on a seat inside to greet us? A childish scream of delight rudely interrupts this thought, as a small boy and girl run past to take their place on the train. Mums, Dads, Grandpas and Grandmas also take their seats on this Saturday family outing.

The conductor, dressed for the day in the original British Columbia Electric Railway uniform, points out proudly the original fittings inside the carriages before telling us the itinerary for the afternoon. Today we will be taking a gentle journey to a halt called Sullivan, going in the New Westminster direction, a return trip of about nine miles.

With the clouds from the forest fire not yet dispersed, the views may be disappointing I fear – there'll be no sight of Mount Baker yet again today. As we chug along to Sullivan halt, what I can see out of the window is an unremarkable rural scene.

We pass fields and blueberry farms, cross rivers and streams, with those gaunt fir trees on the horizon and telegraph poles stalking the landscape, one not that different from the Milner I saw yesterday. I see a few single-storied houses en route, all brick-built now. They are modest enough but still twice the size of that bungalow William stood by at

No 19799 56th – the one which I am sure now had been built on the footprint of the shack where his mother and he stood for the photographer nearly a century ago.

That photo comes back to my mind's eye again, as we travel at a sedate pace through the countryside. Cousin Jessie is unsmiling and looking ill at ease in front of the camera; her eyes half-closed, whether against the sun's glare or the camera's flash. A working woman, briefly interrupted from the day's labours, she stands in her plain cotton dress with its long skirt. Her small boy Willie, or should I call him Bill, is dwarfed by the tall grass – such as I see through the window now – so you can only see the boy's dungaree top and his shirt, seemingly handmade of the same material as his mother's.

Behind them, stands the shack with its chimney, two glazed windows and a small porch. An old bicycle lies on the ground, alongside some planks of wood in a disorderly pile. The wood pile must have grown and grown over the years, so that Mrs Worrell called it to mind as the distinguishing characteristic of Bill Underwood's home. In the distance a small stand of skeletal pine trees reinforces the forlorn air of the scene – those ghostly pines I see on the horizon now.

That photograph was taken at the start of their fifty years in that place together. The decades rolled by.

First come the 1920s, when Jessie had to raise a child alone – the decade between the wars we call the Roaring Twenties, for fun, flappers and excess, and in the States speakeasies and Prohibition.

Then comes the collective hangover, the Great Depression of the 1930s, when Jessie could, no doubt, have done with the windfall inheritance from her natural mother, Mary Ann, which she is unlikely to have ever received. How could she have done, when she had disappeared without even a proper forwarding address and changed her name, not once, but twice?

Then came the 1940s with another world war to live through; her son, maybe exempt from military service by doing farm work. By the second half of that decade, with the war over, Jessie, had reached her late sixties but with no State pension yet provided in Canada had little to give her real peace or security. I've seen a post-war census where she's recorded as keeping poultry, while her son is no longer a farm labourer but a worker in a concrete factory.

As we trundle along on our Saturday pleasure trip, I know for sure now that Cousin Jessie's Langley prairie experience was no rural idyll.

We come to a stop at a level crossing, where the old railway line meets the road. The cars have precedence here now, just as the modern city has been built around the motor vehicle. I doubt Jessie ever learned to drive but she would have seen her home town changed irrevocably by the cars and the trucks.

If anyone came to visit her in the little house on 56th Avenue, they might have judged her a rather forlorn old lady, with no grandchildren to give her joy or to take on outings, her entire family, her bachelor son. Well, the only family she knew that is.

The small boys and girls on the seats near me now have their faces pressed close to the window. They are waving cheerily at the people in the cars at the crossing.

I wave too but Jessie and William have disappeared.

Langley, the next day

Sunday morning and Lorna has another invitation for me.

The weather forecaster says it's going to be a lovely day, warm and sunny. Would I like to go with her husband and her to the seaside this afternoon? It's not far to a little resort called White Rock. It's one of their favourite places for a Sunday afternoon outing, she says.

That will be lovely, I say. When will they be going?

Not till after lunch, if that's ok.

Perfect. That gives me time to do some work before we go out.

I want to focus this morning more on William – or rather Bill – than on Jessie. I have been disturbed by the picture I am now building of him. It's not just from the conversation with Mrs Worrell and my bewilderment as to why he failed to properly honour his mother's grave, it's all the clues there are in the documents from the OPG, that I am now going through.

Firstly, there is a letter dated June 7, 1995 from an archivist at the Langley Corporation to the OPG. This is part of the court file because it confirms that there is no deed poll record of William ever changing his name formally from McDonald to Underwood.

I knew that was an accepted legal route to change identity

or affiliation. Yes, you could do that in England too. I knew that well – very well.

This official-to-official letter also records that George Underwood purchased three graves, for himself, for his wife and his 'adopted' son, probably in 1921 just before he died.

It is a third piece of information though that intrigues – and concerns – me.

The archivist says of William:

'We do have some very old court records, but generally misdemeanour offences dealt with by the local magistrate.'

I know that it's pretty common for young men to get in trouble and 'misdemeanours' were hardly major crimes. Still, it wasn't going to enhance the boy's – or Jessie's – reputations with the neighbours. It also increases my apprehension that William could have been a troubled teenager, perhaps with mental health issues, or possibly, what we now call learning disabled, like my old uncle who was looked after by Mum's spinster sisters.

I wonder, if Bill was disturbed by losing his father-cum-grandfather figure George so soon. The trauma surely was compounded by having to move house for the second time from the city to a village, then from a comfortable farmhouse into a shack, and all before he was eight years old.

There is another document, that gives away more information than I expected: Jessie's Registration of Death signed on June 17 1970 by William as informant. The large looping scrawl *'Underwood'* – just that, no first name – suggests that William's handwriting and probably his general literacy was very poor. The handwriting is notably poorer than his mother's despite those years at Milner school.

The information he provided the registrar was worrisome too. I see that he states Jessie's date of birth as the 28th of January, 1877. Correct month and year (although not the one in his mother's immigration record of course) but the wrong day. Did he really not know his mother's birthday?

He states Jessie's occupation as 'Household duties, at home'. Date she last worked in that occupation, he declares as June 4, 1970, less than a fortnight before she died. Then, it's stated that the total number of years she spent in that occupation was 'Life'. All those years when she worked before William was born, and through his childhood, didn't count then?

Then follows the Medical Certificate of Death. This was signed by the Coroner in early July. It seems there was an inquiry into Jessie's death only completed a fortnight after she was buried in Fort Langley. It's not clear why it took place, as it doesn't seem there was an accident, nor surgery, so maybe it was a sudden death.

At first I read the handwritten cause of death as pneumonia but I look more closely and see it is a condition called 'pneumonitis.' I have to look that up.

It turns out it is a disease often associated with rural work, especially working with poultry and with timber. A sort of industrial disease you could call it then for someone whose only occupation her son describes as 'household duties, at home'.

Maybe William hadn't called out the doctor before his ninety-three-year old mum died. I knew many people hesitated to call for medical help when it cost money to do so. Still here is evidence that the son might have failed his mum at the end.

There's more to think about in the typed transcript of the conversation that the elderly Bill had with his carer in the 1990s (not the handwritten one where I had noticed the reference to his 'mother'). Through these pages emerges a vivid picture of a confused and cantankerous old man. I also discover from this record that he was nearly duped into selling his property for a derisory sum to a man I'll just call J.

Maybe it was a case of dementia, but there's evidence here that Bill had needed care for a long time. There's a reference to a Miss Hughes who it seems looked after his affairs for some years before she had died.

I think back to the words of the OPG manager in Vancouver last week, when he talked of the file he was showing me not being the full one they had. Maybe the authorities – including the social services – knew about Bill Underwood for a much longer time than I thought.

I wish I could have talked to Mrs Jenkins about it. I did check the telephone directories in the library to try to find her but I drew a blank. Hers was not an uncommon name, and she might well not even live in the area any more.

The picture I am getting is that Jessie's burdens as a mother might well have been rather more onerous than most. Whether Bill was her natural son or not, I am sure she would have been a loving mother – but how loving was her son in return? I think of that unmarked grave again.

I stir myself and make one last call. I ring Mrs. Ryan again and tell her that John Jasper Underwood was her great-great uncle. I had time in the library yesterday to recheck the Underwood clan. As I thought JJ was George's brother.

I urge Dawn to contact Kobi so she can take a look at the photograph of the mystery young girl in the *broderie anglaise* white dress. As her mother, Anne, was born in 1905, and visited Milner from an early age, I think that George – even Bill – might have wanted to keep a picture of her.

I am not convinced though from Dawn's cautious response that she will be up to the effort involved in visiting the archive. I put the phone down and feel frustrated again.

Cousin Jessie seems to be slipping beyond my reach here. I might as well enjoy the sunshine and head out with Lorna.

White Rock, B.C, 2017

We are walking along the promenade by the long, sandy beach, which is packed with weekend visitors. There are echoes of the English seaside here, with a pier and people fishing off it. Overlooking the beach, there are pretty holiday and retirement homes, half-hidden by trees and shrubbery. It's quite hot, as the sun is now blazing.

I see in the distance, as if hanging suspended in the air, the outlines of a white peak. I screw up my eyes to try to see more – could it be snow-topped already?

'Mount Baker?' I venture. Lorna confirms it is indeed.

At last I see the 'hoary peak' in Washington State, the one I had read about in that 1883 Directory and which George,

Jessie and William would have gazed on. The Langley which Cousin Jessie had known might have gone for ever but at least this mighty but evanescent mountain remains. I am sure it would have served as a regular reminder to Jessie of that first journey she made across Canada through the even mightier Rockies – and of her always elusive dream.

I have been invited unexpectedly by family of a British friend of mine to visit upcountry. They want to show me the mountains, Lake Louise and Banff. It is an irresistible invitation. Who knows, in this uncertain world, if I would get another opportunity to go there.

I have decided to return to Vancouver a day earlier than I'd planned and then the following day catch the Greyhound bus upcountry.

For the rest of this trip at least, I will put Cousin Jessie behind me.

Sidmouth, Devon, 1970

Maybe it's the disappointing weather, maybe it's just my mood but I am finding this holiday pretty boring. I know in my heart that it will be the last holiday I'll want to take with Mum and Dad, but I daren't let on yet. Walks along sedate seaside promenades, especially in the rain, pall now.

I am worried how they will get on after I've left for Oxford in the autumn. Mum's already given up her office job with Mr Francis. Something she said to me, suggested that Dad wanted her to leave it.

The thought crossed my mind that he was nervous of my mum's transformation. She'd even taken to wearing make-up again. Was it conceivable he was jealous of other men seeing her, now she'd regained her good looks? Surely not. Still, how will they get on when they have only each other for company?

We are staying in a caravan park, as we've done now for the last few years and Dad is talking of saving up to buy a caravan of their own, which he can tow on the back of the Cortina. It might take a few years to save up the money but he hopes they can achieve his dream before he retires. It's hard for me to tell how keen Mum is on that idea, but she'll go along with it, no doubt.

I don't think too much about their future though at the moment. I've just got to get through this wet fortnight in Devon and count the weeks till I can start my new life at Oxford.

I expect I'll keep up with a few of my schoolfriends, but most of them, I think, I'm unlikely to see again. The last day at Wyggeston Girls' certainly felt like the end of an era.

We'd thrown away our navy and white school outfits and were kitted out in fancy dress. We knew whatever we said or did today, whatever we wore, if we well and truly let our hair down, we were beyond risk of rebuke from Miss Pedley.

We paraded down the Regent Road outside the school, singing, cheering, and being generally louder and ruder than we were usually allowed to be in school hours.

We have a new version of Teddy Bears' Picnic for the occasion, written by one of my school fellows which goes:

End of term for Wyggy girls,
The little Wyggy girls are having a lovely time today,
Drinking, smoking, flaunting wares,
For they are craving for a holiday.
See them gaily gad about,
They love to twist and shout
They never have any cares.
At 3o'clock (or half-past two if we're lucky)
Their boyfriends are coming to take them home to bed,
Because they're tired little Wyggy girls.

The man from the Mercury (pronounced Mare-cri in Leicester's vernacular but which I pronounce with three syllables Mur-cure-ee) has come to take our photographs. We cheer some more and pose by our banner declaring our impending liberation from school strictures.

We are 'All Right Now' as the current No.1 single by the band of the moment, Free, declares. Free indeed we feel, as the spirit of the Sixties has intoxicated us.

It's not just me that cannot wait to escape what I think of as a pretty dull Midlands city – not that I have had much opportunity to see its brighter side. Most of my friends, though, are rather better prepared for the real world than I am.

They know I've been what they call 'over-protected'. They tell me 'I'll go wild' when I leave home.

As I sit in the caravan now, I don't really fear 'going wild' as I think the habits of my childhood are too deeply ingrained for me to shake them off quickly. Still, the prospect of going to parties, going out when I like with whom I like – and a boyfriend or two. That – rather than the history course – is what I am looking forward to now.

I know that as well as home, I am leaving my parents behind me. Be careful what you wish for they say. Mum and Dad wished for this outcome so fervently but there is a cavernous rift growing between them and me.

I know when I leave for Oxford, although I will come back to Leicester in the vacations, my heart will move elsewhere for good.

Chapter Fourteen

Huntingdon, 1995

It's all about to make sense.

I haven't given much thought in recent years to my strange childhood, except to be determined to give my own two daughters a happier one than I had. That was a prime driver to our move to the country a couple of years ago.

Howard and I hoped that rural life with a village school plus ready access to open fields would offer our two girls a healthier and freer life than would be possible in London. We'd also wanted to be within easier reach of our two mothers; mine is in her late seventies now, living alone, still in Leicester, with increasingly fragile mental and physical health. Instead of a long drive up the M1, I could now get over to see her within an hour.

Mary's been a widow for getting on for twenty years now. My dad, a heavy smoker, as well as passive smoker for most of his working life, died of lung cancer in 1977. He was only sixty-two and never got to enjoy his retirement. Mum has been a constant source of worry ever since.

Mum and Dad had not had a very settled life after I left for Oxford. They made their first move less than a year later. So instead of the privately-rented house in Knighton, they went to their first council flat – although as they insisted, a very untypical one.

It was the penthouse of an apartment block close to Victoria Park. Maybe the rent was still too high, or maybe they didn't adapt to being on the tenth floor, whatever they soon moved again to a smaller flat on the first floor of an older block not far from my old school.

It was here that Mum was left alone when Dad died. At least and, at last, Mum got to know one of the neighbours there. They even shared the odd cup of tea in each other's sitting rooms.

Still Mum struggled. She had no social life in Leicester to speak of. A visit to one of her sisters was about the limit of it. She also became increasingly concerned about security and a few years ago moved into sheltered housing on the opposite side of the square.

The friendship with her neighbour didn't survive the move, so I worry once more about the loneliness and isolation of her life. She never ventures into the communal lounge.

The move didn't end her security fears; she has become obsessive, putting more and more locks on her front door and refusing access to the social workers who take an interest in her. Her small studio flat is chaotic with a clutter of papers on every surface and discarded clothes on the floor.

Worse, there is little food in the fridge and the place seems cold. I am afraid she is neglecting herself.

Eventually, we persuade her GP to go to see her and within hours she is in hospital. Chronic anaemia is diagnosed.

She is also referred to a psychiatrist. Seeing her in hospital reminds me of the breakdown she had when I was a child. This time though the specialist recommends medication and doesn't hesitate to call her disease by its proper name –

chronic depression with some paranoia.

The hospital tells me that Mum will not be able to return to her flat and needs to go into care. I am provided with a list of care homes and told I have to find a place for her to go as soon as possible so that she can be discharged.

Looking down the unfamiliar list – I hardly know Leicester now – I see one place that might work. It's some miles outside the city, but it's the place her oldest surviving sister is living.

Aunt Lizzie is only a couple of years from her centenary, nearly twenty years older than Mum, but it will be a comfort for both of them, I reckon, for Mum to join her there. There's only a shared room available at short notice and with a stranger, not her sibling, so not ideal, but in the time I have it is the best option.

In my mother's enforced new home, there is little room for anything but the basic essentials. So that's how I come to find myself with the task of clearing my mother's small flat over one weekend. The council will only start helping to fund the care placement if they can reclaim it.

I have little choice but to put her furniture in storage for a while and take everything else in bags and boxes to my house. I remove piles of papers wholesale.

So here I am today sitting at my desk going through them, trying to identify anything important from the detritus of years of Mum's hoarding. I arrive at a large unlabelled brown foolscap envelope.

I remove the contents carefully and place them in a small pile on top of my desk. Much of what's inside are further envelopes, some with postmarks dating from the early 1950s.

Firstly, I see, Dad's death certificate. That's the most recent document and the only one I have seen before.

I open those in the old envelopes carefully one after the other and here's what I find:

A will – my father's, dated 1956, when I was a small child, leaving all his estate to me. I believed my Dad had died intestate.

Several birth certificates, mine. These are a different size and shape from the small square one Mum had given me twenty-five years ago. The first of these is long, narrow and dated early June 1952, a few weeks after I was born.

At a first glance, I can't see anything exceptional about this but it does, for sure, lay to rest the thing I worried about when I was ten years old. I was not adopted. My father's and mother's familiar names are on the certificate.

Then there's another birth certificate, this one in an A4 format: still handwritten but dated to the 16th March 1976, the best part of a quarter of a century after the first. I read this to see what's different from the first one.

Date and place of birth are the same: a Leicester hospital. The name of my father is the same. His occupation has now changed from 'technical representative for furniture manufacturers' of the first to the 'local government officer' he had become. Mum's name comes next.

Then I notice something. There's a line for Mum's maiden surname and it's Chesterton – not McDonald. I go back to the first certificate and I see what I had missed before: mother's maiden name given there too as Chesterton.

In another envelope, comes the explanation and the proof: a deed poll changing my mother's name irrevocably from McDonald. She's kept the covering note too. It's addressed to her as Miss Chesterton from a Leicester solicitor and is dated February 1952.

That was mystifying rather than shocking but then comes this: Mum and Dad's marriage certificate. It is not dated to the 1940s, nor the 1950s.

No, the wedding did not take place until February 1976, less than two years before Dad's death and a month before the date of the second birth certificate. The ceremony was held at Leicester Register Office and witnessed by my uncle Ted and his wife.

It was a wedding I knew nothing at all about of course. That was shocking enough but there was more to come.

I notice a single word against my dad's name: widower. The implication of that single word hits home. Dad had been married before!

He had a wife I had no intimation of and who somehow had prevented Dad marrying Mum till the year before he died. Who was this other woman?

I reel in my seat.

I remember that period in early 1976 all too well. I had been working at the BBC for less than a year, and I took some compassionate leave when Dad became ill and went into hospital. I went to visit him there and he told me that he had lung cancer and that the prognosis was very poor. He had surgery to remove most of one lung and was unlikely to survive more than two years.

He also told me that he had kept this prognosis from mum. He didn't want me to tell her either. He didn't think she'd be able to cope with such news, he said. He asked me to keep this dreadful secret from her, while, as is now dawning on me, at the same time keeping an equally momentous one from me.

I quickly but carefully put these incriminating documents back into their envelopes, then into the bigger one, and put that back in the drawer. I turn the little brass key in its lock and take it to its hiding place nearby.

Truth… will…out, I slowly intone to myself. Here on my desk it just has. An unexploded bomb has lain uncovered for years in a drawer in a Leicester flat until I blithely transported it here to my house in the Cambridgeshire countryside.

I shall have to take care now. The bomb has as yet only been partially detonated.

Cambridge, 2018

It's a few months since I came back from Vancouver and I still can't let Cousin Jessie go. My trip far from bringing closure has opened up in me a new determination.

I am disappointed that I have not heard anything more about the photographs I left in Fort Langley for the community history group. The only news Kobi Christian has had for me is that Hugh Davis, the old farmer I had spoken to on the phone, died just a few weeks after my return.

It makes me realise that as every year passes the chances of my hearing any more first-hand information about Jessie and William becomes more and more improbable. Still, I will keep on checking online sources, as new material gets posted regularly, especially from that First World War period. I will also continue to read whatever I can find which might help me better understand her life.

In one of the books I have ordered from Canada, I am struck by a familiar photograph of a Victorian couple. I know I have a copy in my ever-expanding Jessie file. Until now, I have not been able to identify it.

It turns out it's a picture of the Reverend Dunn and his wife. He features in this history book as the first Presbyterian minister on Langley Prairie.

It must have been George who had a copy of this photo, then it passed to Jessie after his death. I take it as a signal not to give up yet on finding out more of the missing pieces of their story.

I have started to write up my notes to try to form them into a coherent account of my investigations. As soon as I do, I know that I can't hold back any longer from telling my own story – and my mother and father's too.

I feel the final barriers have been lifted, not just by my investigation into Cousin Jessie but also because the last of my parents' generation has passed on – a generation that would have been nervous, even appalled, by putting such a story in the public domain.

Uncle Ted died at the age of ninety-nine last year. I never did get the chance to show him all the photographs I had from my trip to Halifax, Nova Scotia.

Still I console myself that I had had the opportunity in the years before he died to talk to him about his wartime experiences. He sat alone in his sitting room with me and we talked about those – and about Dad. Every time we did,

Uncle told me how much he liked my dad, or GK as he called him. He said it in such a way, as if others might not have done.

Ted had been in the merchant navy, travelling the world, with many a tale to tell. I enjoyed hearing them but it was what he knew about my dad's army service which was more compelling.

He said Dad had seen terrible things. Even now Uncle Ted spared me the full details, but when he said part of his work was to recover damaged tanks, with their dead crew still inside, he did not have to.

In that generation, men could speak man-to-man in a way they could not, would not with women, let alone children. It wasn't done to boast or to 'share' as we call the unburdening of our hearts and traumatised minds now.

I did not hold that against Dad. It was the way things were. Still, keeping his marriage to Mum a secret from me – that was different, that rankles.

Somehow, I still couldn't come straight out and tell Uncle I knew now about Dad and Mum's belated marriage. Maybe I didn't want to betray my feelings about the discovery.

I approached the subject instead very laterally. I thanked Uncle for his friendship to Dad and also for one special favour I knew he had done for Dad and Mum. From his expression alone, I knew he knew what I was referring to – and he realised I knew the truth now.

He nodded but didn't explain. Even now he wasn't going to betray the secret Dad and Mum shared with him – a secret never to be told.

You see he must have known why Mum and Dad had

waited so long to get married – and why some might not approve of his friend GK because of it.

Kingsway, London 1996

So here I am in my office lunch hour in the GRO, the General Register Office, in London, in Kingsway close to the Aldwych. I have what I am looking for in one of the old leather-bound files.

Here it is: a marriage between my father and a woman called Nellie Pegg, in January 1936, at a Leicestershire register office. Dad was just twenty years old, his bride eleven years older. The marriage was witnessed by the bride's sisters. There was no evidence that anyone from Dad's side of the family had attended the ceremony.

I stand stunned surrounded by strangers scanning the pages of the registers. A few lines handwritten sixty years before shake me to the core.

What to make of this? What does it say about my father's backstory? His character?

Just as his war service had been something he never talked about, his life before that war was also something closed to me. Mum told me he'd been very close to his mother and that she'd died very young. His father was never spoken of – beyond one childhood tale of helping his dad out, by carting home coal with him at the time of the General Strike in 1926.

Was this marriage the source of the rift with his father? Or the apparent abandoning of Nellie after the War? Or had they been estranged earlier?

Maybe my dad married this older woman to get away from home after his mum had died. Nellie was described in the marriage certificate as a worker in a children's hosiery factory, living in a village a few miles away from his own. Who knows how they had met.

I am now compelled to consider another possibility: that it was a shotgun marriage and that Nellie had been pregnant. That thought certainly gives me pause.

Was I about to learn of a half-brother or sister that I never knew about? How would I – the only child – who'd longed for an older brother feel about this possible discovery?

I weigh this thought in my mind and decide to keep my anxiety to myself. I've told no-one beyond my husband about the first revelation – that I was born illegitimate. His light-hearted reaction had disinclined me from telling him about my fears around the discovery.

So you're a bastard then, he'd said.

I know that it was meant as a joke and to convey that the revelation meant nothing to him and should mean nothing to anyone else these days. Of course, he was right but he didn't know me when I was a child. He'd never met my dad nor really understood quite how odd and scarring my childhood had been.

My friends didn't know anything about my upbringing either. I wasn't ready yet to share my secret with any of them.

My two girls were still too young to really understand the implications of my family secrets. I didn't say anything to them either. My biggest fear was that they wouldn't be able to keep themselves from asking their grandma about it.

I tell no-one about my plan to investigate another Leicestershire archive. I consult the files again with even more trepidation.

I feel sick and my chest feels as if gripped by a vice. I try to keep my breathing slow and steady as I go through the files of birth registrations for both 1935 and 1936.

I find nothing whether in the name of Pegg or Chesterton. The grip on my chest relaxes. Relief surges over me. There are no secret half-brothers nor half-sisters.

Then I need to confirm when Nellie Pegg died. I have a pretty good idea now when it will have been.

The answer soon emerges from another leather file. Yes, it was only a matter of weeks before the date of my father's second marriage in 1976.

Nellie Chesterton it seems was my Dad's lawful wife for forty years. She lived just a few miles from where Dad lived with Mum, without seeking or being granted a divorce, carrying her married name to her grave.

Of course, just a few years after my father married her, the Second World War broke out, disrupting millions of settled lives. My father did not join up immediately but by 1943 he was enlisted in an army engineering regiment.

When he finally returned from Germany at the end of 1946 he would surely have been a changed man. He was no longer the youth barely out of his teens who'd married a woman a decade older than him and whose whole life up to then had been bound by the triangle of Leicester, Coventry and the small towns and villages in between.

Nellie too may have got used to making the best of her life

alone. By the end of the war she was into her forties and so unlikely to have children. Maybe it was a separation by mutual consent. Maybe it was more brutal than that – perhaps Dad simply never went back to her after the war.

When, I wondered, did Mum learn that the love of her life was a married man? Divorce was not an easy matter especially for working class people in those days. It cost money for a start.

I remember now that Mum had made this very observation to me years before when I was still a child. I think when there was something in the paper about the Duke and Duchess of Windsor, who was, of course, famously a divorcee. I never thought for a moment that Mum was referring to her own situation.

It certainly explained to me now why they left Leicester for a while and seemed happiest at that time. It was surely the return to my mother's home city when she was expecting me that was more surprising.

Wouldn't the McDonald clan have wondered why there was not to be a wedding? Or did my mother come back with a new married name and a ring with a little diamond on her finger (which she wore till the day she died) telling a tale of a quiet register office wedding in Buckinghamshire?

More likely, I felt, she told her brothers and sisters the truth and risked their disapproval or even ostracism – the risk of being disowned, for the shame of 'living in sin' and with an illegitimate child to boot.

Maybe that's why Uncle Ted was at such pains to tell me he always liked my dad. He must have recalled what was said about the affair at the time.

The questions continue to cascade through my mind. How had my father known Nellie Pegg had died? Wouldn't my mother be the only person to know that – when could I ask her?

She was recovering well now from her latest breakdown and had settled well at the care home. It felt the wrong time. Given that any conversation would open up the whole Pandora's box of deception that my parents had created, I decided I had to wait for Mum to initiate the opening up of that box.

In the meantime, I could not help but speculate on the sequence of events in early 1976. I doubt the Pegg family would have had either the desire or the wherewithal to track my father down and tell him the wife he'd abandoned had died.

My father kept no contacts with his own family, apart from a very tenuous one with his sister Rene. I doubt she would have had his current telephone number or address.

I had met her just a couple of times, years ago, when we lived at the Working Men's Club. I felt it was unlikely she'd been the one to bear the news that his wife had died – she still lived in the same area but why would she have kept up any contact with the Peggs?

The most plausible scenario I could think of is this one: as Dad was an assiduous reader of the Leicester Mercury, including the daily birth, marriages, and deaths columns, he had simply read his wife's death notice there. He'd certainly learnt about the death of his own father a few years before that way. I remember that.

I could imagine the relief my father would have felt that he could at last make an honest woman of my mother – yes, that was the phrase that was used. After his cancer diagnosis, he would have wanted to act quickly as well.

I satisfied myself with this conclusion. Life with its normal busyness – the daily demands of work, family life, village life, social life, and the rest of it took over my thoughts and energies again.

I could wait for the day that Mum might decide to start a difficult conversation.

Cambridge, 2018

That day never came.

Mum took what she knew to her grave. It was a secret never to be told.

I often wonder now why I didn't raise the subject when I could with Mum. Tell her I'd found everything out – and that it was ok.

I suppose I didn't quite trust myself not to vent my anger and frustration that they hadn't opened up to me, when I was a grown woman. I would have been shocked of course but I'd still have loved to help them celebrate their wedding.

Mind you, I suspect there wasn't much in the way of celebration that February day when Mum and Dad got married at last, with Dad, knowing he was going to die but not sharing that secret with the woman he'd lived with for thirty years.

Nowadays belated marriages between couples who have lived together but never married and where one party is terminally ill are commonplace – and are wonderful if heart-breaking affirmations of love. Instead I feel that Dad and Mum would have seen their trip to the register office as a simple tidying up of their affairs, conducted in as much secrecy as their previous visits to the solicitor's offices just a stone's throw away.

Then, came the second trip to the same office by Mum a few weeks later: no doubt equally pressing and equally secret. That was to re-register my birth, to make me legitimate at last.

I now realise that there were two Legitimacy Acts of 1959 and 1976 which finally allowed children like me to have a post-dated regularisation of our status. It was one of the many liberalising reforms of that era, most of them better known, like the Abortion Act, the ending of capital punishment and the legalisation of homosexuality.

I've also learnt that the short-form birth certificate I had been given as a teenager was the product of these reforms. They were designed to provide some cover for women who'd had children out of wedlock.

One thing Dad never got around to was having his will re-written. His cancer pretty quickly debilitated him.

I recall now a visit Mum made to a solicitor shortly after Dad died the following year. It was the very same firm which had witnessed that will nearly a quarter of a century before. I had given Mum a lift to the old lawyer's quarter of the city, thinking little at the time of her need to consult a solicitor about probate. I do remember being surprised that she wanted to go alone.

Now I think she must have gone to ask whether that document still had validity – a will which left his widow nothing. I realise now that in 1956 when the will was written, leaving everything to me, Mum was not Dad's next-of-kin. It was Nellie.

This will, made shortly before Mum and Dad briefly owned a house together, was not only Dad's affirmation that I was his child but also a way to keep his assets within his new family. It dawns on me now that even though Mum was apparently excluded from any benefit, it wasn't about disinheriting her but his wife, Nellie.

I think that solicitor must have told her that the will, written in the 1950s could safely be forgotten. Dad had left savings of less than £10,000 and no property. He had even sold his beloved car before he died.

I had no problem at all with Mum having the benefit of those savings. That was only right.

If Mum had ever got around to talking about the events of 1952 and 1976, yes, I would have had plenty of questions, but I would have reassured Mum that everything was alright. I was not ashamed nor censorious. It had all worked out.

Still, I could not trust myself with finally initiating this conversation. I wouldn't have been able to hold back from telling Mum that her life could have been different and not scarred by shame – that my childhood didn't need to have been blighted – that mixing with children my own age in my own street would not have done me – nor my prospects in life – any harm.

I suspected that Mum still felt her sacrifices were justified as I had the life she wanted for me. We didn't argue, the two of us – but I think we would have argued over this choice she made – to live a lie and devise for her only child a strange stunted childhood built on fear and deception – and on snobbery as well.

Maybe, I as a child of the Sixties couldn't imagine quite the level of opprobrium that might have been directed at Dad, a married man, living with another woman who had borne his child. That most of the opprobrium would have landed, not on him but on Mum. The scarlet woman, the bit on the side, no better than she ought to be, living in sin… those are the sort of words that would have been used, wouldn't they?

Whatever, I could have, should have told Mum one thing: that I knew my childhood was grounded in love. That was what really mattered surely and why, ultimately, I thrived.

There was one other reason for my staying silent. It proved a turning-point for Mum after she had that second breakdown. With proper medical care, and with the non-pharmaceutical tonic of company from carers and fellow-residents at the home, she not only recovered, she began to thrive.

Her improvement continued when she moved into a care home closer to our house. My children who had never known anyone other than the sad old woman, who lived in her cold and chaotic flat, fearful and anxious, finally had a grandma to cherish.

There was a golden decade in her life, rivalling I hope those carefree days, when she was a young woman, before I was born. I did not want to risk destabilising that by telling her what I knew.

Maybe she guessed – as she knew I had access to all her papers. Even more reason for me to stay silent, I reckoned, in respect for her decision to say nothing.

Those last years of her life gave us all happy memories of her. Like the hot July day when we threw a surprise ninetieth birthday party for her. My daughter picked her up from the care home and brought her into the garden, where her family awaited: Uncle Ted and his wife, her one surviving sister and nearly all her nieces and nephews were there.

She beamed at us all and we cheered as she cut her birthday cake. She was the happiest we'd ever seen her. There's a lovely photograph to bear testament.

Now more than a decade on from that happy day, one of those who was there, one of my cousins meets me in a café. She's eight years older than me, and so when I was a child I saw her almost as a grown-up. She was already at university when I was ten years old and first had intimations that something wasn't right about my childhood.

Now I don't get to see her very often as she lives in a distant part of the country. So today I summon up the courage to just come straight out with the question.

Did she know that my mum and dad weren't married when I was a child?

She did. She said that everyone knew.

Well, of course, not everyone, in the sense of wider society. No, she was referring to the adult members of Mum's family. As I was almost the youngest of my generation in that family, it effectively meant that I was the only person from whom this secret was kept.

She went on to say that her mum, one of my long-dead

aunts had thought this was the reason Mum had her breakdown back in the 1960s. Out of shame.

Shame, yes that was certainly part of it, but it wasn't the whole story. You see, I think what links the lives of Cousin Jessie, Mum's and mine are the corrosive effects of class and snobbery as well as illegitimacy and shame.

Yes, of course, my Canadian cousin's early life in Cambridge was determined by the circumstances of her birth and the decision to give her away because of that. Yet my trip to her adopted country had led me to conclude that it was only partially the shame of having an illegitimate child – a child that might well not even have been her own – that determined her fate there.

It was also because she was seen as an uppity servant, inveigling a man of means twice her age to marry her. A woman of suspicion, coming out of the blue from the city to a prairie village. A woman who had a dream – of becoming a woman of independent means, leaving her old identity behind and making something of herself. A woman who ended up alone with a 'strange man's boy' – but who despite this, did achieve at least a version of that dream.

As for Mum, thinking about her unhappiness through my childhood years, I am sure it was partially the class difference between Mum and Dad that caused it. Dad enjoyed his job at the working men's club. He enjoyed being a bus driver too. He'd enjoyed the camaraderie of men like him in the army. He was at ease with himself, in a way that Mum never was – at least until that last happy decade.

So instead of joining Dad's world, Mum retreated from it – and did all she could, to make her daughter a proper member of the middle classes, educated, confident and secure, everything she couldn't be. She achieved her dream too.

Chapter Fifteen

Cambridge, 2020

I t has been the most glorious spring – but a silent one.

I am at home and I am surviving in a plague year. I have managed not just to keep the virus away but my spirits up, until recently without the joy of human company.

Yes, I am in contact with my younger neighbours who have offered to do shopping for me. They leave a bag on the doorstep and sometimes I see them to wave at, even to exchange a few words with, by chance when I go out for my daily walk.

Yes, I have seen family and friends through a screen, for sure. I have seen my fellow choir members as we are conducted through our weekly Zoom session. Yes, instead of going to the theatre, I can stream plays into my living room. Indeed, I receive virtually daily invitations to view concerts, talks, every kind of performance online.

It keeps me going, but it is not the same without the press, the buzz, the scents of human company. Don't try to convince me otherwise.

You see, I have known self-isolation and social distancing before, a long time ago. I have spent much of my adult life escaping it.

I have spent the past five years since I moved to Cambridge, building up a new life as a single woman again, a widow, even a merry one at times. I knew a handful of people here when I arrived, none a buddy. I threw myself into the task of creating a new social circle here.

Quite a few people called me brave for that. I felt I had no option. In good health and with the prospect of a third of my life still ahead of me, I was not going to stagnate, rattling around in a cold house in a small village, where life changed little and new experiences would be hard to find.

I was determined to avoid the sort of widowhood that Mum had had – at least until her later years. It was company in the care home that was one of the best tonics for Mum. I knew too well from her experience how corroding to the soul a life of self-isolation and social distancing could be.

Now that the lockdown has begun to lift, there are more and more people, in larger groups, out and about, enjoying the sunshine. To be honest I am not enjoying my daily walks quite so much.

You see, seeing families playing together and groups of flatmates, their cycles on the ground, forming a protective wagon around themselves, laughing, joking, playing music and drinking beer, I feel more alone. I become more impatient to spend time with my children and the friends built up over half a century, who all live a train or car ride away.

I yearn to go to the station, buy a ticket, board a train, get off at King's Cross, or Totnes, or Glasgow – see a friendly face waiting for me there and throwing our arms around each other. I yearn to make lunch in my kitchen for a friend who's travelled to see me. These are acts of friendship and companionship which I have learned to savour only since adulthood; things taken for granted and which we all now understand are more precious than rubies.

After Mum passed ninety, the more sociable life she had begun to enjoy once more melted away as friends in the care home passed away and her own mental faculties start to fade. As she spent more and more time alone in her room, I feared the old demons might return to her.

When I visited her, her mood was unpredictable and sometimes she would be fearful and anxious. One day, she started talking about a walk along a riverbank with her younger sister. Her description was so vivid, it took me a while to realise she was describing something that happened when she was about eight and her sister just a four-year-old. It seems there was an accident and her sister slipped into the water. The terror of her baby sister drowning, while she was in charge of her was as vivid in my mother's mind as if it were yesterday.

On another occasion, I found Mum outwardly calm, as she told me, in a matter-of-fact way, 'Your Dad's just left.'

I knew it was better, if you could, to go along with a loved one's demented thoughts. I paused as I wasn't sure quite what to say.

Then she continued. 'I think, he's left me for another woman'.

I was dumbstruck but felt I had to say something. I reassured her that he hadn't.

Then, I couldn't stop myself saying that Dad had been dead for many years. Mum seemed to accept it and said how glad she was to see me, even though it had been too long since I had visited her.

I came just yesterday, I protest. We moved on to the safer

subject of her grandchildren.

I thought about this afterwards and even more as I have been recalling my childhood recently. I am sure Mum's mind had taken her back to that flaming row when I was a teenager and Dad had left for a couple of days.

I doubt there was ever another woman involved. I don't believe he ever saw his wife after the war. To me, this and the story of her sister's accident betrayed Mum's two deepest fears. – that she would lose two of her loved ones and that it would be her fault.

Mum has been dead a decade now. She died peacefully in her care home, ministered to by cheerful, unmasked and familiar carers, with daily visits from me in the days before she died.

She died less than an hour after I left one evening. That upset me but I comforted myself that she wasn't alone at the end. She had been spared that uniquely 2020 horror, a socially-isolated death.

I am thinking of her this morning as I pass Cambridge's War Memorial on my morning walk. It stands in front of the railings of the closed Botanic Gardens.

Wreaths from last November's Remembrance Day are still there, with their plastic poppies blazing red in the Spring sunshine. On the stone column are inscribed the names of those local men who died in the two World Wars. It is topped by a statue called The Homecoming, and it was the return of her brother Hector, from the First World War which was my mum's earliest memory.

For the past few years, we've heard much about that inglorious conflict, with every grim centenary from early in

2014 to the Armistice commemorated. Yet I don't recall there being much said or written, let alone commemorated, of the pandemic which ravaged the world with martial ferocity at the tail end of that war, in 1918.

We hear plenty about it now. The so-called Spanish flu, I read, took more than fifty million lives worldwide, many more than Covid-19 is ever likely to and now it seems more relevant to our lives than the war which overwhelmed it in the history books.

It sets me thinking. When I had been researching Cousin Jessie's life in Canada, I had thought about her first few years there, very much in the context of the First World War. Among the history books I had read to give me background information about her story was one which framed the whole first half of the twentieth century in terms of conflicts, during what it called 'Canada's turbulent years'. It devoted one hundred pages to the First World War.

I learnt there how Canada, still very much part of the British Empire, had had no choice but to send its young men and some women to a European battlefield. It informed my thinking of how Cousin Jessie's life in New Westminster and in Vancouver might have been impacted during those years.

I get that book down from the shelf, and search the index for Spanish flu. I look in vain. So maybe Canada was spared the pandemic, which I was sure had hit America?

I put 'Spanish Flu Vancouver' in the online search bar and instead of a blank, I find thousands of results. I click on one of them from a website I haven't encountered previously in my research.

Vch.ca turns out to be the web address of Vancouver

Coastal Health. An article from 2018 is headlined '100 years since BC slammed by Spanish Flu pandemic'.

The article opens on my screen and a black and white photograph confronts me with an uncannily familiar scene. Three men in working clothes, their faces covered with cotton masks stand facing the camera.

I scroll down and there is a second picture: of a hospital ward, with a doctor taking a note, a nurse making up a bed and a male porter placing clean linen on a trolley. It was taken in Vancouver General Hospital circa 1919. Then below comes a bar chart, recording the bare statistics of the lethal path influenza took through the city between October 1918 and March 1919.

Vancouver Coastal Health which it seems is the British Columbian equivalent of Public Health England, published this commemorative piece just eighteen months ago when they could have had no idea it would assume a savage new relevance now.

I read on:

'In October of 1918 British Columbia was in the midst of the worst influenza epidemic the world has ever seen... Soldiers returning from World War 1 on trains from Eastern Canada unwittingly helped spread the virus to BC where it thrived in logging camps and First Nations communities as well as towns and cities...

The virus was deadly for otherwise healthy people with strong immune systems. Most of the deaths were among those aged twenty to forty-nine years.'

Its impact on working-age adults rather than the elderly set Spanish Flu apart from the coronavirus. This older pandemic had other differing characteristics too. While Covid-19 takes time to lay its victims low, the Spanish flu could be shockingly fast in its lethality.

'The virus worked so quickly that its victims could be seemingly healthy in the afternoon and dead by the next day.'

That seemed more akin to the sorts of plagues and sweating sicknesses of sixteenth and seventeenth-century England I had read about in my student days and in the historical novel about King Henry VIII's court I have been reading this year. This seemed such a medieval horror to afflict the twentieth-century western world.

This article goes on to describe the limited tools available in 1918 to the physicians and scientists to deal with this influenza virus. I read that in Vancouver in the autumn of 1918:

'Public health officials ordered people to stay indoors and not to shake hands or kiss. Schools, churches and other gathering places were closed to try to stop the spread. Masks were not readily available.'

A lockdown and a shortage of P.P.E. indeed.

Then comes the grim final sentence.

'An estimated 4000 people died in BC from the 1918–19 pandemic – about a quarter of those in Vancouver. In today's numbers that would be about 37,000 deaths for BC and 5000 for Vancouver.'

I close the screen and realise the import of this information. Why had I not known this before? I chide myself.

Cousin Jessie lived through this pandemic, along with her small boy. In the autumn of 1918 I believe she lived with him in Vancouver. She was forty-one years old, within the most vulnerable age group, bringing up alone a three-year-old, also susceptible to this terrible disease. Trying to earn a living, struggling through a winter, where she was forced to stay indoors: wasn't this devastation rather closer to home for Jessie than the war in Europe?

Then comes another thought, no more than that, a moment of revelation.

1919 was almost certainly the year that Cousin Jessie and William left Vancouver for Langley Prairie. It was the year she made a life-defining decision, to leave city life behind and move to the country. Was it, I wonder now, the answer at last to the conundrum, the unsolved question, that still nagged me? After surviving what might surely have been the most challenging winter of her time in Canada, even the most challenging of her life, with no certainty that the plague would not return in a third or fourth wave, had Jessie decided she had to escape?

I see her again, by the lamplight of that side street in Vancouver East: the woman in the grey full-length dress with an anxious expression, her packed bags in her hands. She closes the door and goes down the steps, with little Willie clutching her hand tightly.

I see them walking the short distance to the station.

They board the red and black liveried train of the British

Columbia Electric Railway.

The little boy is excited, his mother nervous. I see her watching out of the window till the city is far enough behind and she sees the landscape changing to a rural one.

She gets out at Milner halt, marshalling the lad carefully off the train. The boy is anxious too now.

They walk up the Trunk Road, stopping at the farmhouses along the way, asking for work. No-one has anything to offer.

Then, as they are getting weary, a white-haired man comes to his farmhouse door. Come on in, he says.

Let me make you a cup of coffee. I could do with a housekeeper.

Now, what's your name?

Mrs McDonald, the stranger replies.

That's a good name, he says. When I first settled here, I had a neighbour called McDonald…Alexander – a fine man and a good farmer. Might you be related?

Cousin Jessie is embarrassed. She mumbles her reply.

No, she doesn't think so. She doesn't have any family here since she lost her husband in the war.

She changes the subject as quickly as she can and sets out her experience to her prospective employer. I can cook, I can clean, I can sew. I've worked for a doctor and a dentist back in England and helped out at the hospital in New Westminster.

The farmer, or George as he now introduces himself, nods. He has no doubt this is a good woman.

He looks down and addresses the boy. I could be doing with some help around the farm. Are you up for that, wee man? he asks Willie.

The boy clings to his mother's skirts. He is pale and thin and George thinks he could do with some country air and some decent food.

Jessie explains that it was for the lad's health and her own she's left the city. George who thinks all sorts of evil lurks there, not just contagious disease shakes his white mane at the troubles the city folk have had over the winter.

George beckons the boy to the door and points to the field outside. He invites the lad to go out to play while he sorts out a few details with Mrs McDonald or Jessie as he insists on calling her. They watch as the lad, let off the leash outside, runs around and around in circles in delight.

George invites Jessie to sit at the kitchen table. She looks around and sees at once that there will be plenty of work to keep her busy. Never mind. She's not afraid of hard work.

The farmer tells her he can't afford to pay her much but there'll be free bed and board.

Deal? Deal.

George puts his hand out to Jessie and she accepts it nervously. In the city that gesture of greeting has been forbidden this past winter.

Can a simple, normal, wholesome life be hers here? Can Jessie dare to hope that she has found a place of safety at last?

This new narrative forms itself readily in my mind – but also the next chapter. Surely the arrival of this strange woman from Vancouver, alone but for a small boy, into a rural community might have caused a stir. Their suspicion of Mrs McDonald was more understandable now. Someone arriving by train from the city, in 1919, might have been bringing more than an illegitimate child with her.

I sit at my kitchen table elated at my latest breakthrough. No, I can't prove it but for me it is the missing link at last – and another curious way in which Cousin Jessie's story makes me reflect on mine.

All of my shared story with my distant cousin must be reframed again through the prism of the pandemic. The virus subtly inveigles itself into the substance of my memory.

I think back to how my story started, as a ten-year-old, sitting in my parents' bed, sick with the measles. Yes, that and the torture of the curtains closed day and night – for fear of going blind.

How my early years were punctuated with childhood illnesses, even though I couldn't remember most of them. Mum told me the worst one was the whooping cough when I had nearly ended up in hospital.

Yes, I can remember another torture of trying to avoid scratching my chicken pox spots. How I did take the top off one of them, leaving an irritating scar.

Yes, I also recall when sitting at Mum's knee in the sitting room of the house next to the club, how she told me of the children at her school who succumbed to T.B. How, indeed, my Uncle Ted had fallen ill with this very disease after his war service. How Mum told me Dad and she had continued to visit him even when others, including in the family, avoided the contagion.

When I went to grammar school, I remember the schoolfellow who was disabled by polio. Then when I was thirteen, how Mum withheld her permission for me to be inoculated against T.B – the BCG I think they called the jab. She was an early anti-vaxxer, long before the word had been coined.

So, yes, infectious diseases and the fear of them impacted on my childhood, right enough. No doubt, when I think about it now, my mum's fear of contagion from disease may have been another compelling reason to keep me well away from other children as much as possible.

Cousin Jessie too would surely have wanted to shield her precious only child from the unhealthy city air and overcrowded places, when she boarded that train to Langley Prairie. She would have been so much more alert to the risks of contagious disease than ever I was – well until this year that is.

From her Victorian childhood onwards, the shadow of life-threatening illness was close by. I think now of Mabel Porter, recorded in Jessie's birthday book, a young domestic servant dead by the age of twenty.

I also remember that Jessie's first port of call in Canada was the quarantine station on the St. Lawrence river. How her first sight would have been the memorial cross to those immigrants who never made it.

The Spanish flu epidemic of 1918, now rescued from historical obscurity, can take its proper place in Cousin Jessie's story at last. In the past couple of years, new insights keep revealing themselves, none as big as this, but still ones that make me reassess Jessie's story.

I still find myself trawling through the box in my kitchen, to see if there are any clues there which I have not yet unearthed. There are still tiny missing pieces of the jigsaw to put together.

I had not paid proper attention to two postcards, addressed to Mrs Jessie Underwood and dating from 1945. They contained a couple of tax assessments from the Langley Corporation, the equivalent of our council tax notices. I had overlooked them, as I assumed they would not yield any new information.

Wrong. These cards referred to Jessie's property not by street or house name, but by lot, block, quarter, and section number. I had assumed they both referred to the 56th Avenue property in a form of office code.

One day I decide to look up the British Columbian land registry website and realise that these coded references are essential to unlock information. The only trouble is that only accredited researchers could use the site. I took a chance and paid a fee to a professional researcher in Canada to find out more about the ownership history of the property.

This researcher tells me that he can provide only basic information about the land ownership, not of the buildings upon it. I realise this means, I won't find out when the shack was demolished.

Despite his caution, he comes up at once with a revelation. The postcards referred to two places not one. From the 1920s on, Jessie owned two separate properties in Langley – how had she managed that?

Soon the researcher has more news for me, first, about the property I do know about, the one I have visited on 56th Avenue. Jessie Underwood had bought this property in 1922 for $900. This was half as much again as the figure that her son told a carer he thought it was worth in 1995.

I worked out that this was the equivalent of about $13,000 in today's money, or by another measure, about three times the average working woman's annual income at the time.

How had such a woman who had arrived as an immigrant just ten years before, with the equivalent of $25 in her pocket, accumulated this sort of level of savings? She would have had to pay cash. I don't believe mortgages were accessible to women back then.

Then my Canadian researcher tells me about the additional acre. That was in a completely different part of Langley and Jessie had bought it for $60 three years later in 1925. It seems she had money to spare when she left Milner.

The most likely explanation was surely that the Underwood Walkers had come to a generous settlement with Jessie to get her out of the farm. I am reminded of the harsh words of George's sister to my cousin about the will which 'you knew would be of no use'. Maybe it turned out to have been a useful bargaining chip for her brother's widow. I am sure if there had been a court record of a formal agreement, the OPG would have found it. So maybe it was an informal arrangement: a generous cash payoff to a housekeeper.

The second one-acre plot bought in 1925, the researcher informs me was sold in 1956 for $440 – a nice piece of capital appreciation, if not quite on the scale of the 56th avenue property. Had Jessie bought it as an extra acre to keep chickens or grow vegetables on? Or maybe Jessie was planning ahead – thinking of somewhere she – or Bill – could have moved to, if her boy ever married and needed a place of his own.

By the 1950s, she'd have realised that was not going to happen. Now an old woman with her middle-aged bachelor son still living with her, it would have provided some additional cash to draw on. It's a comfort to realise that Jessie might not have missed that £40 left by her birth mother as much as I had feared.

Although I have to draw a line now under Cousin Jessie's story, the door will always be open for new revelations and new perspectives. I know too that the techniques I have used to recover her from the past, I can also use on my more immediate family.

When the UK Census taken in 1939 became publicly available online recently, I learned exactly where Dad lived with his wife Nellie at the outbreak of war. I also see Mum's name listed at her parents' home in Leicester.

I've gone through Dad's Army records recently too, trawling every detail. The VE Day 75th Anniversary this year gave me the impetus.

I had another shock in store. Dad was still in the territorial army in 1956 and even at that time continued to declare Nellie as his next of kin. If anything had ever happened to him while on duty, it would have been on Nellie's door that the Army would have come knocking not ours – and remember, Dad talked of going back into active service around that time when the Suez Crisis left him unemployed.

We have to confront our own histories and then come to terms with them. My luck – in receiving the windfall inheritance, then in becoming custodian by chance of Jessie's mementoes, began my quest to understand three women's lives, Jessie's, Mum's and mine. The way the cards fell for me propelled me onwards, to unlock secret lives and to understand at last my own childhood and how I had come to be the person I became.

I will finish this story with one more curious discovery. You can call it a portent – or a strange coincidence. It was hiding in plain sight, not amongst Jessie's box of mementoes but amongst my mother's.

I had to do a big clear out when I left my house in the country five years ago. Those things of my mother's that I had not disposed of but put into a cupboard emerged again. Of course, those extraordinary documents, the deed poll, the will, and all the rest were amongst them. There were also a few pictures.

There was a watercolour drawing in a rather heavy wooden frame of a young Victorian woman. My mother had always liked it and it had, I understood, come originally from her family home. I decided to keep it even though there was no space for it on the wall of my new house.

I put it away in a new cupboard but it took up too much precious space to stay there long. I decided that the only thing to do was to remove the ugly frame and just keep the print.

I carefully extracted it so as not to damage the picture. I turned it over and there for the first time was revealed some writing in pencil on the back.

I could not believe what I saw.

I reached for a magnifying glass to make sure that my obsession with Cousin Jessie's story hadn't turned my head. No, it really did say:

Mrs Rook of Cambridge.

I looked at the portrait closely and yes, it did indeed bear some resemblance to the much older woman captured in that Victorian studio photograph. The clear blue eyes were the same, for sure.

Had this portrait of Jessie's adoptive mother somehow been passed down from William Heading via John McDonald to his brother, my grandfather? Who knows?

All I knew is that in this moment of revelation, I saw it as another sign that this was the story I had to write, the truth I had to tell. There really was just one degree of separation between my mother and Jessie Underwood, aka McDonald and nee Heading.

May they both rest in peace.

Appendix

Acknowledgements

T hanks are due to very many people who helped and encouraged me in researching and writing this book. I should like in particular to acknowledge the enormous help and support I have received from librarians, archivists and amateur – but expert – local and family historians in Cambridge, London, Dumfries and Canada.

Cambridge is a great place to start a family history project; there are so many knowledgeable enthusiasts. I should like to thank in particular Mike Petty, for his initial guidance, including in helping decipher Victorian photographs. He was the founding father of the excellent local resource called the Cambridge Collection, hosted at the Central Library, which was invaluable for me in recreating Jessie's early life. Another Cambridge stalwart, Mary Naylor, also helped set me on my way.

In Canada, I found help and a friendly face everywhere I travelled, in Halifax, Nova Scotia, in Vancouver Public Library and the archives in New Westminster, Cloverdale and Langley, B.C. I should like to give a particular thank you to Kobi Christian, to Nancy Josland Doslin and Fiona Weston.

In writing the book, I received support from many friends – you know who you are – and from my daughters, Sarah and Rachel. I would not have written this book at all, without the support of the people I met through an Arvon Foundation writing week in 2018 at the Hurst in Shropshire. This creative writing charity really did inspire me and thanks are due to Lois Pryce and Ian Marchant in particular. Our group met regularly after the course and I thank Meriel Schindler for organising our get-togethers.

I should also like to thank Ben Dunn who gave me professional support in preparing my submission to publishers. He encouraged me to tell more of my own story, which was challenging for me, not just because of my upbringing but because as a former journalist, it didn't come easy to put myself at the heart of the story.

My thanks above all are due to James Essinger for offering to publish this, my first book.

As the book makes clear, I conducted a lot of detailed historical and genealogical research. If I have made any mistakes, particularly in telling the Canadian side of the story, I apologise. This has not been undertaken as an academic exercise, nor to scholarly standards, but I have always tried to be fair to the evidence I have uncovered.

Notes and References

Throughout, I use information from the General Register Office's records of Births, Marriages and Deaths, the UK censuses from 1851 through to 1911 and similar data from Canadian sources. These can also usually – but not always – be accessed online by searches of commercial sites like Ancestry.com. Much of this information can also be found directly at the British National Archives, www.nationalarchives.gov.uk and its Canadian equivalent, www.bac-lac.gc.ca.

Chapters One to Three: Cambridge Research

While the first breakthrough on Jessie's father was through a digital record accessed in the Cambridge Collection room at the public library, I also visited the Cambridgeshire County Archive to confirm this baptism record, Calm KP22/1/5; P22/1/5.

The collection of Spalding's directories for the period of my study was essential in providing useful information between the ten-year censuses and in understanding the town where Jessie spent her early life. These are also in the Cambridge Collection.

The detailed research, carried out by the Friends of Mill Road Cemetery in cataloguing the graves and in gathering stories about the people buried there, helped me tell the story of Ebenezer Canham.

I also used a very informative local website called CapturingCambridge.org. It was here that I learnt more about the Drake family, who ran 'The Cav' stores and featured in Jessie's birthday book.

Information about Charles Darwin came from Christ's College website, www.christs.cam.ac.uk.

I am grateful to the librarian at St Catherine's College, Sarah Fletcher who answered questions about the Silver Street house where Mrs Rooke and Jessie lived in 1901. Harriet Rooke's death registration confirmed she was still at this address in 1912 and described her as the widow of Alfred. (Cambridge district, vol3b520). At the time of writing, I can find no record of where Harriet is buried.

Chapter Four

Punting as we know it started in Cambridge early in the twentieth century with Jack Scudamore founding the company that still plies its trade down the Cam and its backwaters: https://www.scudamores.com/history-of-punting.

The photograph of the Yanaluk family, by William Topley, can also be found in the digital collection of the Canadian archives, www.bac-lac.gc.ca.

Jessie's immigration record is held in the national Canadian archive under this file: Immigrants to Canada, Porters &

Domestics, File Title: Commendation Register, Canada No 12, Girls' Friendly Society Fund. MG28 1-349, vol. 67, p 34, microfilm reel A-1196. (See also chapter 5 note).

I calculated that the $25 that Jessie is recorded as bringing into Canada would have been the equivalent of £15 at the time. One way of understanding its value is to compare this sum with the wages of domestic servants in the early twentieth century which according to a variety of sources seems to have varied from £20 to £40 per annum according to seniority. As Jessie's wage would have been at the lower end of the scale, £15 was a considerable sum for her to have saved.

There is useful background on the experience for immigrants arriving at Quebec in an essay by Robert Vineberg available from the Pier 21 archive. https://quai21.ca/sites/default/files/uploads/files/QuebecCity-byRobertVineberg.pdf.

Details of the sinking of the Ionian Steamship can be found at uboat.net. More about the Allan Line including passenger lists and other information are held inter alia at the websites, shipslist.com and norwayheritage.com.

There were different shipping routes for ships travelling from Britain to Canada according to the season. It is probable that the route the Ionian took from the Port of London via Le Havre to Quebec was the Spring and Fall St Lawrence route via Cape Race.

Grosse Ile was established as a quarantine station in 1832 following a cholera epidemic. The Library and Archive Canada website has an article on its history and also includes a search facility to trace people who were treated and died there: https://www.bac-lac.gc.ca/eng/discover/immigration/

immigration-records/immigrants-grosse-ile-1832-1937/
Pages/immigrants-grosse-ile.aspx.

Chapter Five

The records of the Girls' Friendly Society are held in the
Women's Library at the London School of Economics.
Commendation register No1, dates the start of the emigration
scheme to Canada to 1907 (Box no. 139, 5GFS/04/06).
Annual reports of the GFS, including emigration reports by
the Hon. Mrs Joyce are in Box no. 120 5GFS/03/035/
036/037.

Commendation Register No.12 (Box no. 141 5GFS/04/067)
includes the record for Jessie Heading.

Cambridge Branch Reports 1890–1916, 5GFS/06/038, in
Box no. 170 records Jessie's membership between
1910–1912.

The Girls' Friendly Society survives but is now a very
different organisation, which you can read about at https://
girlsfriendlysociety.org.uk.

Chapters Six to Fifteen: British Columbian Research

I made much use of the searchable database of British

Columbia City Directories at https://bccd.vpl.ca, held physically at Vancouver Public Library.

Chapter Six

Jessie's address in New Westminster is in the 1913 edition of Henderson's *Greater Vancouver Directory*, Part 2, New Westminster.

Her possible Vancouver address under the listing Jessie McDonald, widow, at 1840 7th Ave East is in the 1915 Directory at page 794, In the following year's edition, she is listed at page 749.

I checked First World War military records available at https://www.bac-lac.gc.ca/eng/discover/military-heritage/first-world-war/personnel-records/Pages/personnel-records.aspx, to try to find a Mc or MacDonald from British Columbia who might have died in service. This is now complete, but was still in progress in 2017.

Chapter Seven

The Sillitoes, Acton Wendever, the first bishop of New Westminster and his wife Violet are well-documented in Canadian sources. They arrived in British Columbia from

England in 1880 shortly after their marriage. Violet Sillitoe wrote a pamphlet entitled *Pioneer Days in British Columbia*, a copy of which is in the library of the Queens University in Toronto. A biography of Violet (1855–1934) is at westendvancouver.wordpress.com. Henderson's *Greater Vancouver Directory* for 1912 lists Violet Sillitoe at 1860 Robson Street. According to a record held in the Anglican Diocese of New Westminster Archives, Violet was 'beloved throughout the province'.

Chapter Eight

I read about the history of the Royal Columbian Hospital especially its expansion in 1914 from *A Call to Nurse: Memories of Life on and off Duty in a Hospital Training School 1901–1978*, pub Royal Columbian Hospital School of Nursing Alumnae Book Committee (2013).

The frequently poor experiences of domestic servants arriving in Canada in the early twentieth century is set out in a collection of articles edited by Franca Iacovetta, with Paul Draper and Robert Ventresca, *A Nation of Immigrants, Women, Workers, and Communities in Canadian History, 1840s-1960s*, University of Toronto Press, 1999.

The New Westminster Museum and Archives also provided me with other useful background material.

Chapter Nine

George Underwood arrived in Canada in 1878. The Great Depression in agriculture is widely referenced in historical books and articles e.g. Richard Perren's *Agriculture in Depression 1870–1940*, CUP, 1995, and in P.J.Perry's *British Agriculture 1875–1914*, Methuen, 1973. This accounted for much of the internal and external emigration from farming communities in that period.

George is listed as a farmer on the British Columbia censuses from 1881 through to 1911, searchable via https://www.bac-lac.gc.ca/eng/census/pages/census.aspx.

He also features regularly in the directories available at bccd.vpl.ca (see above)

I quote extensively from the Wrigley's Directory for 1882/3, pg255–8. (New Westminster district, Maple Ridge, Langley and Matsqui).

Mount Baker which is first mentioned here is known as one of the snowiest places in the world, setting the world record for recorded snowfall in a single season in 1999. It was well-known to indigenous peoples of the Pacific North West who called it Koma Kulshan. It was discovered by the Spanish in 1790 and 're-discovered' by the British explorer George Vancouver and named after one of his crew, Joseph Baker. It is situated in Washington State, being the third highest mountain there at 3286m.It is visible from much of Greater Victoria, Greater Vancouver and Seattle.

Chapter Ten

I found Mary Underwood Walker's visit from the USA to Milner in 1914 via a search of Ancestry.com. Border entry lists are archived at bac-lac.gc.ca but at the time of writing are not searchable by name.

I am grateful to the Dumfries and Galloway Family History Research Centre in Dumfries for their help in finding the home and final resting place of Margaret Bell.

Since I visited Langley, I have become better informed about attitudes to women's ownership of land in early twentieth century Canada and society's resistance to their becoming farmers in this period. See Professor Sarah Carter's book, *Imperial Plots: Women, Land and the Spadework of British Colonialism on the Canadian Prairies*, University of Manitoba Press, revised edition 2018.

Chapter Eleven

There is an extensive collection of photographs and objects available to search and view at the Langley Centennial Museum collection. (collections.museum.tol.ca). The map of the Hudson's Bay farm surveyed in 1877 is Object ID 1984.095.013.

The British Columbia Census of 1921 (see chapter nine reference) taken around June of that year, three months after

George's death records Jessie Underwood and William still living on the farm on Trunk Road. The handwriting is at times unclear, so William's age of six has been wrongly interpreted elsewhere as sixteen. On the occupation line the original word Farmer is clearly scored out, with another word, apparently Manager, written over.

It is likely that Jessie and William moved to the small property at 56th in Langley township in 1922. However, it was 1925 before the Wrigley Henderson Amalgamated British Columbia directory records George Underwood Walker running the Milner farm (https://bccd.vpl.ca).

My imagined account of Jessie and George's marriage is based on the details in the certificate filed under 1920-09-219649. BCA No: B12905 GSU No:2032874 (Reg No 176/20, also at Reg No 12/7/1920).

Chapter Twelve

Archibald McDonald was born in 1790 in Glencoe, Scotland and left for the Red River Settlement in Canada under the patronage of Lord Selkirk in 1813. He joined the Hudson's Bay company in 1820. became a colonial administrator, fur trader, justice of the peace and surveyor. In fact, the marriage to Jane Klyne, a mixed-race woman was his second. In 1823 he had married 'Princess Raven' the daughter of Chinook Chief Comcomly with whom he had one son as well as the thirteen by Jane (Jean Murray Cole in *Dictionary of Canadian*

Biography).

Chapter Thirteen

Information about Jessie and William's occupations from 1935 onwards came from the Voters' Lists (similar to our electoral registers) searchable at https://www.bac-lac.gc.ca/eng/census/Pages/voters-lists.aspx. William Underwood is described as a farm labourer in the Voters' List for Langley of 1940 and 1958. There is also a reference to his working in a concrete factory and several references to Jessie keeping poultry.

Much background information about life in Langley from the late nineteenth century through to the 1950s is to be found in Warren F. Sommer's book *From Prairie to City: A History of the City of Langley*, Friesens ,1999. It provided invaluable background information, photos and maps including a photo of the Reverend Dunn (see chapter fourteen).

Jessie's death certificate, was registered in British Columbia, No. 70-09-010210.

Chapter Fifteen

My information on the Spanish Flu in Vancouver and quotations come from www.vch.ca/about-us/news/100-years-since-bc-slammed-by-spanish-flu-pandemic

Research of Jessie's Langley property started with the website www.ltsa.ca. I am grateful for Darby research services for obtaining further information from the records of the Land Titles Office on the two properties Jessie owned.

Further Reading

For further general reading on British attitudes to illegitimacy see Jane Robinson's *In the Family Way: Illegitimacy between the Great War and the Swinging Sixties,* Viking 2015. An account of American attitudes can be found in Deborah Cohen's book *Family Secrets: The things we tried to hide,* Viking 2013.

For an accessible, if traditional account of the First World War as it was experienced in Canada see Pierre Berton's *Marching as to War: Canada's Turbulent Years 1899–1953,* Anchor Canada 2001.